REGISTERING
VOTERS BY MAIL

REGISTERING VOTERS BY MAIL

The Maryland and New Jersey Experience

Richard G. Smolka

in association with Jack E. Rossotti

American Enterprise Institute for Public Policy Research
Washington, D. C.

Richard G. Smolka is professor of political science and director of the Institute of Election Administration at American University.

Jack E. Rossotti is assistant professor of political science at American University.

324.2
S666w

ISBN 0-8447-3162-5

Domestic Affairs Study 30, May 1975

Library of Congress Catalog Card No. 75-13545

Printed in the United States of America 78-3736

CONTENTS

PREFACE

This study is primarily concerned with the effectiveness of mail registration in increasing the number of voters who are registered and who actually vote. It also examines the extent to which this system can accomplish the dual objectives of enhancing the voter's convenience and protecting the integrity of the electoral system.

Legislation providing for a national voter-registration agency and for a system of voter registration by mail was introduced in the 92nd, 93rd, and 94th Congresses. Known for its sponsor and vigorous promoter as the "McGee bill,"[1] this legislation was passed by the Senate in 1973 but has not yet been accepted by the House of Representatives. During hearings and debates in both houses of Congress, neither proponents nor opponents of the proposal have been able to adduce any empirical evidence to support their case. Although Texas, Alaska, and Kentucky have made some use of voter registration by mail, until 1974 no state had put into practice a system in which the majority of new registrants was actually enrolled by mail.

Maryland, New Jersey, and Minnesota inaugurated mail-registration systems that became effective during 1974. In the five Maryland jurisdictions with mail registration and in New Jersey, the majority of new registrants actually did register by using the mail-registration form. In Minnesota, however, the law permitted voters to register either by mail or at the polling place on election day and many voters chose the latter option. Thus, Maryland and New Jersey provide the most useful information about the effects of a mail-registration system and are the focus of this inquiry.

In the research for this study, administrative details—such as the distribution and return of the mail-registration form, verification of

---

[1] S. 1177 (94th Congress), introduced by Senator Gale McGee (D-Wyoming).

the identity of the registrant, purge practices, and ballot security—were scrutinized. The cost of administering a mail-registration system was examined. Side effects, such as nonvoting uses of voter-identification cards, were uncovered and these are described here. The role played by the U.S. Postal Service in operating mail-registration systems was also investigated. A special effort was made to distinguish between those effects of mail registration that are intrinsic to the system and those that are the product of administrative variation in implementation.

Primary data for this study were made available by the chief election officials of the states of Maryland and New Jersey and by the county boards of supervisors of elections in Maryland and the county commissioners of registration in New Jersey. Officials in every Maryland county using mail registration and in every county in New Jersey were interviewed. Statistical data were evaluated only after consultation with the appropriate state or local election official. Voter-registration data are particularly dependent upon the methods by which they are compiled and it was extremely important to determine precisely what each figure meant. For example, if one jurisdiction counts a "change of address" as a new registration and another does not count it at all, registration figures for the two jurisdictions in a single year cannot be compared as they stand.

Finally, because both Maryland and New Jersey rely at least in part on the U.S. Postal Service for verification of addresses of voters, one aspect of this service was tested. Both states by law presume that if a nonforwardable voter-notification form is sent to a voter and is not returned, the voter in fact lives at the address to which the form was sent. This address check is one of the security aspects of the system. The test attempted to determine what percentage of nonforwardable first-class mail would not be returned even though mailed to fictitious persons.

Because mail registration has been in effect in New Jersey and in parts of Maryland for such a short time, most of the conclusions of this study are necessarily suggestive and tentative. Nevertheless, certain definite and potential effects of the mail-registration system have been identified.

Chapter 1 supplies the necessary background and explains the terms commonly employed in connection with voter registration in the United States (though the precise meaning of these terms varies somewhat from place to place). Chapters 2 and 3 describe the registration and election systems of Maryland and New Jersey respectively, as well as the administrative structures and procedures connected with registration by mail. The final chapter analyzes the results and presents the conclusions of the study.

During the course of this research, generous assistance was provided by the Maryland State Administrative Board of Election Laws and its administrator, Willard Morris, by Assistant Secretary of State of New Jersey F. Joseph Carragher, and by Gerry Goodwin of the Elections Section of the Department of State of New Jersey. County officials in both states were extremely helpful in providing descriptions of their own systems, as well as election statistics and critical commentary. The authors are also grateful to Charles L. Miller, a graduate student in political science at American University, whose timely comments and supportive research made substantial contributions to this study. In addition, we owe a special debt of gratitude to Mary Wason for her willingness to work long hours under adverse conditions to complete this report.

1
HISTORY AND PURPOSE
OF VOTER REGISTRATION

When communities were smaller and populations more stable, there was little need for voter registration. Most people knew their neighbors, and residents were easily identified even if not known personally by election officials. Doubts were resolved in the precincts on election day. But as populations grew, particularly through immigration, the need to determine voter eligibility in advance of election day became apparent. Fear of the voting tendencies of the new immigrants, as well as rather widespread fraud, led to the adoption of restrictive legislation including voter-registration laws.

In his classic study of voter registration, Joseph P. Harris noted that before the enactment of registration laws "it was not unusual for armed men to appear at the polls and demand the right to vote."[1] These persons were permitted to vote and then, according to Harris, were never seen again. Elections turned into "riot and shooting matches."

Voter registration establishes that the person who offers to register is a citizen of the United States, a resident, and a qualified voter from the address from which he offers to vote. The practice of making voter lists public by printing them in newspapers, posting them in public places, and making them available to political parties and candidates offers an opportunity to challenge persons whose eligibility seems questionable before the election. Finally, at the polling place it must be determined that the person who offers to vote is in fact the person whose name is on the registration list. In some states, the voter's eligibility as well as identity may be challenged at the polling place. The effectiveness of voter-registration procedures as

---

[1] Joseph P. Harris, *Registration of Voters in the United States* (Washington, D. C.: The Brookings Institution, 1928), p. 6.

a fraud deterrent may be ascertained by examining how the list is compiled, how and when it is publicized, and how it is used at the polling place. Harris warned that any weakening of the registration provisions, or the failure to provide a sound system of voter registration, would give rise to election fraud sooner or later in any populous community.

Personal Voter Registration

Almost all jurisdictions in the United States require voter registration prior to election day. The responsibility for being registered rests with the voter, who must apply and satisfy the appropriate local election official that the legal requirements for registration and voting have been fulfilled. The lists of all qualified voters are a matter of public record, though their accessibility and the extent of their use .vary from state to state.

Periodic registration. The first systems of voter registration in the United States required that reregistration take place periodically every one, two, or four years depending upon state law. Any change of name or address made reregistration necessary. The periodic registration system operated on the assumption that it was necessary or desirable to prepare a completely new list of voters for each major election or at frequent intervals. Politically, it was intended to make it more difficult for some people to vote.[2] The periodic voter-registration system was widely used around the turn of the century and remained in existence in many parts of the United States through the 1920s. It was attacked by civic groups such as the National Municipal League and election scholars such as Joseph P. Harris because it was both inconvenient for the voters and very expensive.

Permanent registration. Reformers advocated a system of permanent voter registration. Under this system the voter, having once registered, remains registered until he dies, moves away, or is disqualified from voting. The reasons for disqualification, which are determined by state law, include conviction for a crime, usually a felony, the legal determination that a person is of unsound mind, or failure to vote during a prescribed period. All states with the exception of North Dakota, which requires no voter registration, now

---

[2] For a brief description of varieties of voter-registration systems in the United States as well as other countries, see Richard J. Carlson, *Voter Registration Systems in Canada and Western Europe* (New York: National Municipal League, 1974).

have permanent voter-registration systems. The degree to which the systems are "permanent," however, is directly related to the provisions of the law related to the failure to vote. States which remove the name of persons from the registration lists for failure to vote within a two-year period have not moved very far from the system of periodic registration.

Purges of voter-registration lists. With periodic voter registration, the lists needed few revisions because all voters were required to register during each election cycle. The permanent voter-registration list, however, must be "purged" at intervals in order to ensure that the names of those who have moved away or died are removed. The point on which state voter-registration laws vary most significantly today is the manner in which purges are prescribed and executed. The most common provision specifies that a voter's registration is cancelled for failure to vote in at least one election—special, primary or general—within a proscribed period of generally two or four years; some states, however, purge only for failure to vote in general elections. In a few cases nonvoting is permitted for longer than four years. Another critical factor is the method of removal. In some states a registered voter who has failed to vote receives a nonforwardable post-card. Only if the card is returned to the registrar as nondeliverable is the voter purged from the rolls. In other states the voter is permitted to respond to a notice which automatically reinstates him at his current residence address if it is located within the same jurisdiction. There are almost as many variations in nonvoter purge practices as there are states, and each has implications for the permanence of the registration and for the amount of reregistration that is required.

Several other procedures are employed to ensure that voter-registration lists are accurate. On occasion, door-to-door canvasses are authorized. Certain official government agencies such as courts, bureaus of vital statistics, and health departments may be required to supply the local registrars with lists of persons who have died, been convicted of crimes, changed their names by law or marriage, or been declared of unsound mind. In some states a change of name or address makes personal reregistration necessary, while in others a simple signed statement entitles the voter to remain on the rolls. As with the purge for nonvoting, practice varies at the local level, regardless of the specific provisions of the law. In most jurisdictions more names are listed on the voters' registry than would be there if the law were followed explicitly. If the system is permanent and if there is little attempt to purge the lists, the names of many voters who are no longer eligible—some of whom, in fact, are no longer living—remain

3

on the rolls. These names, commonly referred to as "deadwood," are an administrative burden, cause unnecessary expense, and provide an opportunity for vote fraud.

Many states provide for reinstatement of previously registered voters by mail. For example, in Ohio a voter who has not voted at least once during a two-year period is sent a "voter-registration reinstatement card."[3] If the card is completed and returned by mail or in person to the local board of elections within thirty days of the date of notice, the voter is reinstated. Anyone who fails to return his card is purged and must reregister in person before he is eligible to vote again. The Ohio system is very similar in effect to a postcard voter-registration system for all previously registered voters.

In some states, voters who are registered but who change their address, name, or political party may inform registration authorities of this fact by mail or by completing and signing the appropriate form, while in others they are required to reregister in person. In some states, a person who moves from one town or one county to another must reregister in person but in others the matter is handled by a simple transfer. In each case, the purpose of the registration or re-registration is to obtain an original signature or other means of identification of the registrant and to ascertain that he is, in fact, who he says he is.

Registration Methods

With the exception of North Dakota, each state requires its subdivisions to administer a voter-registration system which includes personal registration in a central elections office. This is usually a county function, and the title of the local official who handles this function is usually clerk, registrar, recorder, supervisor of elections, or election commissioner. Almost all jurisdictions provide for central office registration during normal business hours or at specified times most days of the week. Registration is continuous except for a short period immediately prior to elections, usually thirty days, when the registration books are closed so that officials can prepare current precinct voter lists for use at the polls.

Most jurisdictions also provide for supplementary registration which may operate in any or all of several different ways. Regular full-time or part-time employees of the board of elections may be dispatched to register voters at shopping centers, schools, fire stations,

---

[3] Ohio Secretary of State Ted W. Brown, press release, 3 February 1975.

banks, libraries, or other public locations. Some jurisdictions establish these decentralized or branch locations on a permanent or semi-permanent basis, whereas others use them only in the peak periods prior to an election. Mobile registration vehicles and even trucks have also been used as branch offices for voter registration.

Some states, including New Jersey, authorize or require voter registration at specific times or places during peak registration periods prior to an election. Whether central, branch, or precinct registration locations are established, these are usually manned by full- or part-time employees of the board of elections who have had some training for this work.

Deputy Registrars and Door-to-Door Canvasses. California, Arizona, and some other states authorize the use of deputy registrars who function without pay or who are compensated on the basis of the number of persons they register. These deputies are permitted to register people where they find them whether in public places such as shopping centers or in their private homes. The deputies operate under the general supervision of the appropriate registration official but receive no specific assignments and may be as active or as inactive as they wish. In California a small percentage of deputies register the vast majority of those voters who are registered by deputies.

Systematic door-to-door voter-registration drives, conducted under the direction of local election officials, have been used in Hawaii and in the state of Washington. These drives, like a census, have been designed to reach every eligible person. Although many states authorize house-to-house canvassing for the purpose of purging voters from the list, relatively few authorize or encourage door-to-door canvassing for enrolling voters.

Mail Registration in the States. Since 1942 members of the armed forces have been permitted to register and to vote absentee. A federal law effective that year provided for a postcard application to be used in requesting a military ballot. By 1944, all the states had made provision for absentee voting by military personnel, in some instances waiving the registration requirement or accepting the federal ballot application in lieu of registration. The current Federal Postcard Application (FPCA-Standard Form 76) has been used since 1955 and an ever-increasing number of states have accepted that form for the purpose of voter registration as well as for use as an absentee ballot application. Under current law, any members of the armed forces and merchant marines and their dependents, as well as citizens of the

United States temporarily residing abroad, may use the federal post-card form to apply for absentee ballots.

Texas has used a system of mail registration for some years. Because voter registration in past years was periodic rather than permanent and because payment of a poll tax was required for voting, mail registration did not add greatly to the number of registered voters. Mail registration has not been widely encouraged in Texas, which remains a state with a lower than average voter registration and voter participation.

Alaska permits mail registration for voters living in certain areas where accessibility may be difficult for prolonged periods, especially in winter. The combination of a sparse population, rugged terrain and weather, and large distances has forced the state to adopt methods of registering votes and even of delivering ballots (air-drops to isolated islands) which are unique.

Kentucky adopted a mail-registration law primarily to facilitate reregistration of all registered voters when a statewide voter-registration system was implemented in 1973. The state now permits but does not encourage voter registration by mail. Applications are available upon request from the county clerk's office. By far the greater number of new registrations, estimated by the Office of the Secretary of State to be 50,000 per year, are made in person rather than by mail.

Minnesota passed a voter-registration-by-mail law that took effect in 1974. Prior to this, many of the state's smaller communities had no voter-registration requirement of any kind. In order to avoid disfranchising voters because they had not previously registered, the Minnesota law also permitted voters to register at the polling places on election day. This provision was applied to jurisdictions which had previously required registration as well as to those which had not. The effect of the law was to eliminate voter registration prior to election day as a requirement for voting, and thereby reduce the incentive for voters to register by postcard. Large numbers ignored the postcards and registered on election day instead. In Minneapolis, 14,104 out of the 25,732 persons who registered to vote during 1974 did so at the polling places on election days. The remaining 11,628 used the postcard registration form, which was distributed by political parties and civic groups and was made available in public places such as fire stations.[4] The same form was used for those who registered in person in the office of the city clerk. For these reasons, the

---

[4] Interview by Richard G. Smolka with Lyle Schwartzkopf, city clerk of Minneapolis, Minnesota, January 1975.

Minnesota system does not yet offer a true test of the potential of postcard voter registration.

The Maryland mail-registration law was passed in 1973 and became effective in four counties and in Baltimore City on 1 January 1974. Fifty-seven percent of the population of the state lives in these counties. By July 1975, with the exception of two small counties, every county in the state will have initiated mail registration of voters.

In New Jersey legislation permitting mail registration of voters took effect in August 1974, only a short time before the general election. The program was immediately implemented and succeeded in registering large numbers of voters. The New Jersey law was uniform statewide and permitted candidates, political parties, and civic groups to distribute, collect, and return completed voter-registration forms to the commissioners of elections. Reports from several counties indicate that more registrations were returned by political groups—whose members served, in effect, as deputy registrars—than were returned through the mails.

The Maryland and New Jersey laws are discussed at length in succeeding chapters.

Federal Registration-by-Mail Proposals. Senator Gale McGee (D-Wyoming) first introduced a national voter-registration-by-mail bill into the Senate in 1971. Senator McGee contended that the low voter turnout in the United States compared to other countries where free elections are held was largely due to the system of state responsibility for voter registration. In an effort to eliminate what he called a "confused tangle of registration requirements," he proposed a national voter-registration agency within the Bureau of the Census and a national voter-registration-by-mail program for federal elections. The bill also provided for grants to the states for the administration of the program. The bill failed to pass the Senate.

Similar legislation was introduced again in 1973. This time the McGee bill, as it came to be known, was subject to a filibuster but, on the third cloture vote, the filibuster was terminated and the Senate passed the bill in May 1973. Hearings were held in the House of Representatives and in due course the bill was reported out of committee. It came to the floor of the House from the Rules Committee but was sent back to that committee when a procedural motion to reject the rule was carried by seven votes. No vote on the bill itself took place.

In 1975 Senator McGee introduced his proposal once again, this time with fifty-one cosponsors. In the House of Representatives,

Chairman Wayne L. Hays (D-Ohio) of the Committee on House Administration, which is the parent committee of the Elections Subcommittee, introduced a proposal very similar to Senator McGee's except that the Hays bill placed responsibility for the administration of the mail-registration program in the General Accounting Office rather than in the Bureau of the Census. A freshman congressman, Don Bonker (D-Washington), who had formerly been county auditor in Clark County, Washington and a chief election official himself, also introduced a voter-registration-by-mail bill. Bonker's proposal called for a federal grant to each state to implement its own mail-registration program before a "date certain" by which, unless certain minimum levels of voter registration had been achieved, a federal mail-registration program would be imposed on the state. The prospects for passage of a mail voter-registration bill in 1975 are very strong.[5]

Registration as a Safeguard against Vote Fraud. The relationship between voter registration and vote fraud is simple and direct. Harris found that most of the frauds are made possible by ineffective voter-registration procedures. As he put it, "the corrupt precinct politician sees to it during the registration period that there will be a sufficient number of names on the precinct registers to take care of any emergency which may arise."[6]

Voter-registration lists are padded in several ways. Individuals may fraudulently register, either in their own names or under fictitious names, at false addresses. Sometimes persons may be registered from fictitious addresses but this is less common. In fact, many persons now on voter-registration lists maintain legal voting residence addresses which are vacant lots, shopping centers, high-rise office buildings or superhighways and there is no fraud whatsoever. Such persons are former residents who have moved out of state or even out of the country but who, under state law, are permitted to maintain their former residence address as a voting address even though there is no residence at the address. Legislation has been introduced in the 94th Congress which would secure this legal right for all American citizens residing overseas.

Voter-registration imposters have commonly used the names of actual persons who have died or moved away. During the Senate

[5] See Kevin P. Phillips and Paul H. Blackman, *Electoral Reform and Voter Participation* (Washington, D. C.: American Enterprise Institute, 1975), Chapter 5, for a review of various congressional voter-registration proposals during recent years.
[6] Harris, *Registration of Voters*, p. 11.

debate on the McGee bill in May 1973, Sam Ervin (D-North Carolina) facetiously defended this type of vote fraud against what he feared would be possible under the McGee proposal. Ervin said that, with the old method of cheating, at least there was a "modicum of honesty" —which he illustrated by a story: John Doe and Richard Roe went to the cemetery to copy names off the gravestones and they proceeded until they came to a gravestone which read, "Sacred to the Memory of Isadore Tscherenstein." Richard Roe said, "Wait a minute, that's a long name; we can divide it into two parts and have two ballots instead of one." John Doe replied, "Oh no, if I'm going to have anything to do with this, it's got to be honest!"

This method of vote fraud is declining, however, because the actual person can be identified and/or located by investigators, thus establishing the existence of fraud, though not necessarily discovering the perpetrators of it. Fraud was uncovered in Gary, Indiana, in 1967 and in Chicago in 1972 by locating actual persons whose names and addresses had been used for false registration and/or voting. Signature checks provided the evidence that the investigators needed to support witnesses and obtain convictions. Seventy-five persons were indicted and fifty-seven pleaded guilty or were convicted for vote fraud in the Chicago primary election of 1972.

Evidence of vote fraud is usually difficult to obtain. Discovery may occur after the votes have been cast and sometimes only after they have been counted, when the perpetrators of the crime have long since departed from the scene. Many prosecuting attorneys are not inclined to indict or convict persons for vote fraud, which is only a misdemeanor in many jurisdictions. Although rumors about vote fraud persist in many places, the investigation stage is seldom reached, and indictments or convictions are obtained even more rarely. In recent years there have been instances of convictions or guilty pleas to charges of vote fraud in West Virginia, Virginia, Illinois, Ohio, and California, this last case pertaining to a 1974 congressional race. But these are rare exceptions to the general rule.

Use of Voter-Registration Lists at Polling Places. Voter identification at the polling place is usually accomplished by signature verification. The election judges match the voter's election-day signature with the signature in the registration books. Not all jurisdictions require a signature check at the polls. If an electronically produced registration list is provided and the original registration signature of the voter is not available at the polling place, the voter may be asked merely to state his name and address. If this information matches the computer printout or other form of nonsignature list, the voter may be permitted to vote. In some jurisdictions, judges are instructed to ask for the date of birth or other personal identification if a signature check is not used. Any number of items may suffice for precinct voter identification, including a voter-registration card, social security card, driver's license, birth certificate, credit card, employer identification card, or other commonly accepted means of identification, depending both upon what state law specifies and what the precinct judge or challenger is willing to accept.[7] There is great variation in the manner in which judges seek to identify voters. Some do, in fact, check the identification of every voter. The common practice, however, regardless of state law, is to not verify the identity of the voter beyond obtaining the name and address and confirming that it is on the registry. Usually, unless there is reason to doubt the identity of the voter, the procedure is quite lax. Many states also have provisions for voting for persons whose names do not appear on the rolls. Such persons may be required to appear before a local judge and plead their case or they may be required merely to file an affidavit at the polling place after which they may be permitted to vote a regular or a challenged ballot, as the law provides. In some states, there is no provision for relief and the voter whose name is not on the lists is not permitted to vote. Voting by unregistered persons has been cited in election challenges quite frequently and was in part the basis for a congressional contest of the election result from the Ninth District of Virginia in 1974.

Voter-Registration Statistics

A discussion of the meaning of voter-registration statistics must be prefaced by a few precautionary words. The quality of these statistics varies greatly from jurisdiction to jurisdiction in relation to the stability of the population and the frequency and thoroughness of the purge process. High voter registration does not necessarily indicate that a locality is doing well at registering voters. It may merely mean that it is doing a poor job of maintaining an accurate current list of eligible voters, that it has failed to remove the names of people who have died or moved away. On the other hand, low voter registration may not necessarily indicate that a community is doing a poor job of

---

[7] Office of Federal Elections, United States General Accounting Office, *A Study of State and Local Voter Registration Systems* (Washington, D. C.: Government Printing Office, August 1974).

registering voters. A transient community may have to register very high numbers of voters merely to keep pace with the numbers who have been removed from the rolls because they have moved away. Because the methods and frequency of purges are not the same in all of the jurisdictions within a state and certainly not from state to state, comparisons between jurisdictions and between states must be made only after a clear understanding of *both* the registration and the purge practices has been achieved. For many reasons, voter-turnout figures are presumed to be a more reliable indicator of political activity than voter-registration statistics.

Voter Turnout. Voter turnout is the number of persons who actually come to the polls or cast ballots in a given election. Not all jurisdictions record or report these statistics. Voter-turnout figures usually cited for presidential elections are the numbers of valid votes actually cast for that office. Voter turnout in nonpresidential years is sometimes defined as the number of votes cast for the highest office on the ballot. Voter turnout defined as the number of votes cast for an office is usually at least one percentage point less than voter turnout defined as the number of voters who cast ballots. In nonpresidential years it may be somewhat higher. Even in presidential years, under special circumstances and in some communities or states, a much higher percentage of the population may choose to ignore the presidential candidates and cast votes only for other offices on the ballot. Voter-turnout figures, therefore, must be used with caution. In this study New Jersey reports the total number of ballots cast at an election, including the number of votes disqualified. Maryland, like the majority of states, reports only the votes cast and counted for each office and question. Maryland's total voter turnout is actually one or two percentage points higher than the vote cast for any individual office at the top of the ballot.

Voting-Age Population Eligible to Vote. The voting-age population (VAP) is a base figure used to evaluate both voter registration and voter turnout. Estimating voting-age population for any jurisdiction is not an easy task. Population reports published by the Bureau of the Census are presumed to be fairly accurate for the period in which the census was taken. However, for cities or counties which are rapidly growing or experiencing large population shifts, these figures quickly become outdated. Occasionally a state or municipal government conducts a census which provides a basis for estimating voting-age population for nonnational census years. The Bureau of the Census also provides periodic estimates of voting-age population.

Other estimates are based upon statistics produced by state or local health authorities or planning agencies. In brief, there are many estimates of voting-age population and each is likely to deviate from the others according to the assumptions made in arriving at the estimate.

The voting-age population, however, is not the same thing as the total population *eligible to vote*. Aliens, persons convicted of certain crimes, and those who have been judged mentally incompetent are disqualified from voting according to the laws of the several states. Aliens constitute between 3 and 6 percent of the total population of the country, but are concentrated in a relatively few cities and counties.[8] The number of persons ineligible to vote by reason of conviction for crimes or mental incompetence is not known. According to census reports, 0.5 percent of the voting-age population in Maryland and 0.7 percent of the voting-age population in New Jersey were in mental hospitals or correctional institutions in 1970.[9] Not all of these persons were disfranchised, but not all persons disfranchised were in institutions.

Other factors which affect the relationship between voting-age population as determined by the census and the number of persons eligible to vote include the presence of persons who reside in an area without claiming the right to vote there. For example, a military base or a university may introduce large numbers of people who do not claim the right to vote in the jurisdiction in which the institution is located. Alaska was placed under the Voting Rights Act because fewer than 50 percent of its voting-age population were registered voters, but at the same time or shortly thereafter, the state claimed that it had registered 90 percent of the *eligible* voters. The difference was accounted for by the presence of a very large number of transient military personnel stationed in that state. As another example, several thousand people living in the Maryland and Virginia suburbs of Washington, D. C. and employed by Congress or other agencies of the federal government maintain legal voting residences different from their actual residences in which they are counted for purposes of the census.

There is one additional consideration that is probably more important than the eligible voting-age population in determining the number of new registrations that is possible or likely in any jurisdic-

---

[8] About 4.5 million aliens legally in the country filed their residence address as required by law during the past year. The Immigration and Naturalization Service estimates that there are additionally between 4 and 12 million aliens illegally in the country.

[9] United States Bureau of the Census, *Population Estimates and Projections*, Series P-25, no. 526 (September 1974), p. 7.

Table 1

TOTAL POPULATION AND VOTING-AGE POPULATION IN
NEW JERSEY AND IN MARYLAND COUNTIES
WITH MAIL VOTER REGISTRATION, 1970

County	Population	Percent 18 Years of Age and Over	Estimated Voting-Age Population Eligible to Vote[a]
NEW JERSEY	7,168,164	66.6	4,487,557
Atlantic	175,043	68.6	112,874
Bergen	898,012	68.1	578,853
Burlington	323,132	63.8	193,788
Camden	456,291	64.8	277,935
Cape May	59,554	71.7	40,138
Cumberland	121,374	64.9	74,044
Essex	929,986	67.6	590,949
Gloucester	172,681	62.7	101,773
Hudson	609,266	70.7	404,905
Hunterdon	69,718	65.0	42,597
Mercer	303,968	68.6	196,019
Middlesex	583,813	64.2	352,318
Monmouth	459,379	63.9	275,930
Morris	383,454	63.4	228,522
Ocean	208,470	67.1	131,490
Passaic	460,782	67.8	293,665
Salem	60,346	64.8	36,757
Somerset	198,372	63.7	118,780
Sussex	77,528	62.9	45,839
Union	543,116	68.7	350,734
Warren	73,879	66.8	46,389
MARYLAND	3,922,399	64.7	2,421,793
Baltimore City	905,759	66.4	574,358
Harford	115,378	62.3	68,645
Howard	61,911	60.8	35,947
Montgomery	522,809	63.7	318,042
Prince George's	660,567	62.7	395,537

a This estimate differs from that of total population eighteen years of age and
over by 6 percentage points in New Jersey and 4.5 percentage points in Maryland.
This difference takes into account the nonvoting alien population and persons in
institutions in each state.

Source: U.S. Bureau of the Census, *County and City Data Book, 1972* (Washington, D. C.: U.S. Government Printing Office, 1973).

Table 2

STATE BOARD ESTIMATED VOTING-AGE POPULATION
ELIGIBLE TO REGISTER IN MARYLAND COUNTIES, 1974

County	Estimated Population 1/1/75	Estimate Eligible to Register [a]	Registered Voters 10/7/74	Percent Eligible Population Registered
Allegany	82,600	45,612	40,491	88.77
Anne Arundel	334,000	184,435	125,203	67.88
*Baltimore City	840,000	463,848	389,596	83.99
Baltimore County	650,600	359,261	303,904	84.59
Calvert	25,200	13,915	9,463	68.00
Carolyn	20,500	11,320	7,713	68.13
Carroll	79,300	43,789	27,370	62.50
Cecil	54,600	30,150	20,138	66.79
Charles	59,200	32,690	21,234	64.95
Dorchester	28,900	15,959	12,796	80.18
Frederick	93,800	51,796	37,236	71.88
Garrett	22,400	12,369	10,097	81.63
*Harford	129,900	71,731	51,197	71.37
*Howard	93,100	51,410	41,546	80.81
Kent	16,800	9,277	8,191	88.29
*Montgomery	583,900	322,430	291,280	90.33
*Prince George's	706,300	390,019	215,139	55.16
Queen Anne's	19,500	10,768	8,490	78.84
St. Mary's	51,700	28,549	16,953	59.38
Somerset	18,800	10,381	9,867	95.04
Talbot	25,300	13,971	11,416	81.71
Washington	106,300	58,699	43,379	73.90
Wicomico	57,600	31,807	24,394	76.69
Worcester	26,900	14,854	10,777	72.55
MARYLAND	4,127,200	2,279,040	1,737,870	76.25

* Counties using mail registration during 1974.

[a] Estimate eligible to register is calculated at 55.2 percent of the total population in each county.

Source: All above figures including percentages are from State Administrative Board of Election Laws, *Annual Report to the General Assembly*, February 1975.

tion. That consideration is *rate of growth*. A rapidly growing county has a far greater potential for registration than a county with the same population numerically but with older and more stable communities. In most states all new residents of a county must register in order to vote. The rate of growth or more precisely, the rate of population movement into a county, must be considered in analyzing comparative voter-registration statistics. Failure to have a precise estimate of the rate of growth may lead to erroneous conclusions about factors such as the percentage of the voting-age population that is registered or votes or the comparable performance of jurisdictions in registering voters.

Using population estimates published by the State Department of Health in January 1975, the state of Maryland has estimated voting-age population to be approximately 55.2 percent of the total population in each county.[10] (See Table 2.) Although this rough estimate may be reasonable for the state as a whole, it fails to take into account variations by county. Bureau of the Census estimates of voting-age population are closer to 65 percent of the total population for each state.

Because estimates of voting-age population eligible to vote in each county vary so widely according to the assumptions used, these estimates are of limited utility in this study. See Table 1 above for VAP estimates for Maryland and New Jersey counties with mail registration.

---

[10] State Administrative Board of Election Laws, *Annual Report to the General Assembly*, February 1975.

2
MAIL REGISTRATION IN MARYLAND

Maryland, one of the first states to adopt mail registration on a large scale, is the eighteenth-largest state in the union. Its population was 3,922,399 according to the 1970 census and had risen to an estimated 4,127,200 by 1975. Baltimore City is the largest jurisdiction. The suburban counties of Montgomery and Prince George's in the Washington metropolitan area have experienced phenomenal growth in the past two decades and now have a combined population of more than 1.4 million. Baltimore County, which did not use mail registration in 1974, is the third-largest jurisdiction, somewhat larger than Montgomery County but smaller than Prince George's. Twenty-three counties and the independent city of Baltimore are the basic units of local government in Maryland and have primary responsibility for voter registration. The city of Baltimore is treated as a county for most purposes and is geographically independent of the counties. Baltimore County is a suburban county in the Baltimore metropolitan area but is independent of Baltimore City.

The Maryland Department of Health estimates the population of Baltimore City to have been 840,000 as of 1 January 1975. This is down from the 1970 census count of 905,979. Blacks comprised 46.7 percent of the city's total population in 1970 and are expected to become the majority in the near future. In most respects, Baltimore is similar to other older eastern cities (see Table 3).

One-third of the residents of Montgomery County are college graduates. The county has the second-highest median income of counties in the nation according to the 1970 census. One-third of the work force is employed by federal, state, or local governments.

Prince George's County, the largest in Maryland, has experienced greater population growth than any other Maryland county for several

17

Table 3

POPULATION CHARACTERISTICS OF MARYLAND COUNTIES WITH MAIL VOTER REGISTRATION, 1970

	Race (in thousands)		Percent Negro	Percent Spanish Origin	Median Annual Family Income ($)	Median Education (years completed)	Percent Completed Four Years of College	Percent Owner-Occupied Housing	Percent Employed by Government
	White	Negro							
Baltimore City	480	420	46.7	.9	8,814	10.0	7.2	44.4	20.1
Harford County	57	5	8.0	.8	10,750	12.1	12.9	65.7	32.6
Howard County	12	4	25.0	1.0	13,461	12.4	20.5	76.4	26.2
Montgomery County	495	21	4.1	3.0	16,708	13.0	33.2	61.4	33.7
Prince George's County	562	92	14.1	2.2	12,445	12.5	17.1	50.1	39.8
State of Maryland	3,199	698	17.9	1.4	11,057	12.1	13.9	58.8	25.7

Source: U.S. Bureau of the Census, *County and City Data Book, 1972* (Washington, D. C.: U.S. Government Printing Office, 1973).

decades. It differs rather strikingly from its Washington suburban neighbor, Montgomery County, in several ways. Prince George's has many more blacks, 14.6 percent of its total population in 1970, and these include many natives, of the county and a growing number of former residents of Washington, D. C. Prince George's also has a higher rate of apartment occupancy, a higher transient population, and a younger population (including many school-age children). Located in Prince George's County are the University of Maryland with a student body of approximately 35,000 and Andrews Air Force Base with a military population (including voting-age dependents) of approximately 12,000. Very few of these residents are actually eligible to vote in Prince George's, most being registered elsewhere, if at all.

Howard and Harford counties are in the Baltimore metropolitan area, and both have been growing rapidly since 1960. Howard County has a substantial black native population, but current growth consists largely of white suburban homeowners and residents of new apartments. Howard County's population increased from 36,152 in 1960 to 93,100 by the end of 1974, much of the increase due to the new town of Columbia located almost midway between Baltimore and Washington, D. C. Growth in Harford County, a suburban area northeast of Baltimore, has resulted primarily from migration from that city and from Baltimore County.

Selected population characteristics of these counties and of the state are shown in Table 3.

Maryland's Election Laws

Maryland's laws pertaining to federal, state, and county elections (including elections in Baltimore City, which is treated as a county for election purposes) are specified in Article 33 of the Annotated Code of Maryland, more commonly referred to as the election code. Maryland has a strong tradition of county option, and there are individual county exceptions to several state election laws and practices. This tradition lay behind the decision of the Maryland General Assembly to adopt mail voter registration only in the counties which desired to implement the practice.

Municipal elections in Maryland, with the exception of those in Baltimore City, are conducted under laws entirely different from county and state law. Each municipality is permitted to establish its own voter-registration requirements and procedures. At one time, two municipalities in Maryland had reduced the legal voting age to eighteen years for municipal elections, even though the state constitution provided for a minimum voting age of twenty-one and even though that age governed for all other elections conducted within the state. Some municipalities, for example, the summer resort of Ocean City, provide that property owners may vote regardless of whether they reside in the municipality. It is legal in Maryland for a person to vote in elections in more than one municipality in the same year, even on the same day, so long as that person qualifies to vote in each municipality. Residents of municipalities, with few exceptions, must register with the municipality in order to be eligible to vote in municipal elections, but must also register with the county in order to be eligible to vote in county, state, and federal elections. Municipalities are permitted to use county registration records if they choose to do so, but most do not.

Election schedule. Maryland conducts a primary and a general election every even-numbered year. County and state officials are elected for four-year terms in nonpresidential even-numbered years. Baltimore City conducts its municipal elections every four years in odd-numbered years and will have an election in 1975. Except for this and occasional county or state special elections, there are no elections in odd-numbered years. As noted above, municipalities other than Baltimore City are not bound by the general election code of the state and may conduct their elections at times and with frequencies determined independently of the schedule described above.

Voter-registration requirements. In general, any citizen of the United States eighteen years of age or older, who has resided in Maryland for thirty days preceding a general election and who is a resident of a county or of Baltimore City at the time the registration books are open, is eligible to register to vote. Seventeen-year-olds who will be eighteen on or before the date of the next general or special election are also permitted to register. This permits seventeen-year-olds to vote in primary elections provided they will be eighteen by the time of the general election. Like the law of most states, Maryland law provides that persons who have been convicted of certain crimes or ruled mentally incompetent may not register except under specified conditions. As noted above, these provisions do not necessarily apply to municipal elections.

Election Administration

State Administrative Board of Election Laws. Registration of voters and the general conduct of elections in Maryland is under the general supervision of the State Administrative Board of Election Laws. This board, created in 1969, has five members appointed by the governor with the advice and consent of the Senate. Three members of the board belong to the majority party in the state, the party of the governor, and two members belong to the principal minority party. All members are unsalaried but receive a per diem and expenses. The term of office is four years.

The governor also appoints a full-time state administrator of election laws who serves a six-year term. The first and only administrator of election laws in Maryland is Willard A. Morris. Prior to this appointment, Morris had been responsible for voter registration and elections in Montgomery County for four years. In 1964, while working as a county election official, Morris organized the Maryland Association of Election Officials, and he served as its first president until 1968. He is widely regarded as one of the most knowledgeable persons in the state on the subject of election law and administration.

The state board exercises general supervision over voter registration, but this function remains a primary responsibility of the local boards of supervisors of elections. The state board maintains a current statewide list of registered voters, helps the counties update their lists, approves all forms used for mail registration of voters, and is authorized to take an active role in voter registration and/or the purge process when special circumstances are present. The role of the state board in purging the registration lists in Baltimore City is touched on below (see page 23).

In addition, the state board performs a wide variety of election-related duties. These include processing candidate and treasurer reports, preparing ballots, publishing election returns, and certifying candidates. Despite its heavy responsibilities, the state board functions with a very small staff. It began with only two employees in 1970 and seven were authorized for fiscal year 1975.

Voter Registration. Voter registration in Maryland is the primary responsibility of the boards of supervisors of elections of the twenty-three counties and Baltimore City, which, for the purposes of elections, is treated as a county. In each of these jurisdictions, a three-member Board of Supervisors of Elections is responsible for the conduct of all county, state, and federal elections within the county. Members of the county boards, like those of the state board, are appointed by the governor, who makes the appointments upon recommendations from the local party central committees. Two members of each county board are from the majority party in the state and one is from the minority party. Maryland law requires the governor to notify the local central committees of the majority party and the principal minority party each time there is a vacancy on the board within the county. Each county central committee is required to submit the names of at least four eligible persons affiliated with the party to the governor and the governor is required to appoint one of the persons on the list unless all are deemed to be unfit or incompetent.

Maryland residents must register to vote in person before two registrars, one a member of the majority party in the state and the other a member of the principal minority party in the state—except in those jurisdictions and in those instances where registration by mail is permitted. Registration is permanent: once registered, voters are not required to register again unless their registration has been cancelled in accordance with the law. Registration is continuous and the books in all counties and Baltimore City are open except for the period that extends from the fifth Monday preceding a primary, special, or general election until ten or fifteen days after the election.

Maryland is a "closed party" state and registrants are required to give their party preference at the time of the original registration if they wish to vote in a primary election. Voters who decline to state their political party affiliation are classified as "declines" and are not permitted to participate in the primary elections of either major party. Changes of party affiliation or from "decline" to a political party are permitted whenever the registration books are open, with one exception: no change of party affiliation may be made during the four-month period immediately prior to a primary election.

Use of Registration Lists at Polling Places. Voter identification at the polling place is accomplished by signature verification or personal identification. The prospective voter is usually required to sign his name, which is then matched against the signature in the registration books provided when the voter first registered. Because personal signatures change over time, any similarity between the two signatures is usually acceptable to the precinct judges. In some counties, electronically produced registration lists rather than registration books are permitted in the precincts. In the absence of a signature, judges are requested to verify identity by asking for the date of birth or for some personal identification such as a driver's license. There is great variation in the actual identification practices of precinct officials throughout the state. In some precincts one or more judges have personal knowledge of most of the registered voters, and voter identification poses few problems. Some judges do attempt to check the identification of every prospective voter to ensure that he or she is the person whose name is on the list of registered voters. Other judges will accept the word of a person who identifies himself as a registered voter whose name appears on the lists, unless there is strong reason to question the identity of the prospective voter. Because Maryland law permits challenges only on the basis of identity and not on the basis of voter qualification, there are few challenges to voters. None of the five jurisdictions in which mail registration was used during 1974 could cite any instance of a voter's identity being challenged at the polls during the past five years.

Purges of Voter-Registration Lists. The function of purging the registration lists is a county responsibility in Maryland. By far the greatest number of removals are for failure to vote. State law requires the counties and Baltimore City to remove from the registration lists the names of all persons who have not voted in at least one special, primary, or general election during a five-year period, but in fact the frequency and method of purging the registration books vary from jurisdiction to jurisdiction.

A name must also be removed from the lists when officials have reason to believe that the person no longer resides at the address indicated, or that there has been a death, a change of name, or a criminal conviction. Certain courts and state and local administrative officials are required by law to provide information of record pertaining to deaths, marriages, legal changes of name, and criminal convictions to the State Administrative Board of Election Laws. The state board forwards this information to the county election boards throughout the state. Upon receipt of an official notification which would invalidate a voter's registration, the local election board is required to advise the voter of the information received and to request the voter within fifteen days to show cause why his or her registration should not be cancelled. Between July 1973 and December 1974 the state board processed 43,793 death notices, 36,829 changes-of-name-by-marriage notices, and 54,345 cancellation notices (including those received by Maryland from former residents who had registered to vote in other jurisdictions).[1]

Procedures for Voter Registration by Mail

In 1973 the Maryland General Assembly enacted a law which provided for mail registration of voters in Harford, Howard, Montgomery, and Prince George's counties and in Baltimore City. These five jurisdic-

---

[1] State Administrative Board of Election Laws, *Annual Report to the General Assembly*, February 1975.

tions contained 57 percent of the population and 56.9 percent of the registered voters of Maryland as of 7 October 1974. At the time the bill was being considered in the legislature, either the elected representatives or the election officials, or both, from all other counties opposed the application of the legislation to their own counties.

Voter registration by mail was not new to Maryland. Election law had previously permitted absentee voter registration by mail for specific classes of persons, including members of the armed forces, persons whose physical disabilities confined them to hospital or bed, and citizens who were out of the county during the times when the registration books were open. Such persons were and are now permitted to register in Maryland by applying for and casting absentee ballots. In effect, almost any person who is out of the county or physically unable to register in person is able to register by mail in any county of the state. Thus, the new legislation extended to all residents of the five jurisdictions mentioned above the opportunity to register by mail which had previously been available only to absent or disabled residents.

The registration-by-mail law contained a general grant of authority to the state board to promulgate rules and regulations for the operation of the mail-registration system. The law specified, however, that all information submitted on mail-registration forms should be supplied by the applicant under penalty of perjury. The bill did not change the qualifications for voting in any way. Mail registration became effective in Maryland on 1 January 1974; procedures for implementing the law became operative in Howard and Montgomery counties and in Baltimore City on 1 January, in Harford County on 1 February, and in Prince George's County on 1 March.

Rules. After consultation with the affected counties, the state board established the rules and procedures for voter registration by mail. While retaining the right to approve any mail-registration form prior to its use by any county, the board allowed variation in size, format and style to permit compatibility with the filing and storage systems used in each county (see Table 4). The state board permitted the local boards to utilize mail-registration forms in lieu of the standard registration forms wherever officials conducted registration in person. Distribution of the voter-registration application (VRA) forms was authorized at locations not staffed by election officials, but county controls to protect against frivolous distribution by individuals or groups were encouraged. Counties were permitted to distribute mail-registration forms to groups in bulk, but local boards were advised

Table 4

SIZE AND CHARACTERISTICS OF MAIL-REGISTRATION
FORMS, MARYLAND AND NEW JERSEY

	Length	Width	Self-Mailer	Postage Paid
Baltimore City	11″	8″	Yes	Yes
Harford	15″	8″	Yes	No
Howard	15″	8½″	Yes	No
Montgomery	8″	6″	No	No
Prince George's	15″	8″	Yes	No
New Jersey	11″	8½″	Yes	Yes

not to do so unless appropriate instructions had been given to the groups receiving them, including information about the penalties for violating the law. Cards given to groups had to be code-stamped so that, when they were completed and returned to the election office, they could be identified with the distributing group for purposes of analysis. The rules also prohibited any group from accumulating or assuming the responsibility for returning the completed registration forms. Each individual registrant in Maryland is responsible for returning his own VRA, either in person or by mail. Another rule prohibits any local board's denying one party central committee the authority to distribute registration forms if it permits another party to do so.

All forms used in Maryland counties advise prospective registrants that they must be citizens of the United States, at least seventeen years old and to be eighteen by the next general election, a resident of the county, not convicted of a disqualifying crime, and not under guardianship for mental disability. Voters, by their signature, swear or affirm that they meet these qualifications. The only information actually required is full name, complete address, date of birth, place of birth, and previous registration. Party affiliation is also requested but voters may decline to provide it. Voters are advised on the form that only persons affiliated with a political party may participate in the primary elections of that party. Each form also contains a separate section which must be signed and which serves as an authorization to cancel prior registration anywhere in the country. This section is designed to be forwarded to the county or state where the voter was previously registered.

After the form has been completed by the registrant and mailed to the local board of supervisors of elections, processing begins. The VRA should be date-stamped upon receipt by the local board. Each office has its own procedure for checking for previous registration and identifying the district and precinct in which the residence is located. If the information provided on the VRA form is complete and if the applicant meets the requirements for registration, a voter-notification card is sent by nonforwardable first-class mail. This card contains the name and address of the voter, the date of registration, the ward, district, and precinct in which the residence is located, and the party identification specified by the voter. It also informs the voter of the location of his polling place. If an application is submitted by a voter who is currently registered, the voter is notified of this fact and given essentially the same information provided on the voter-notification card.

The local board is required to conduct an appropriate verification inquiry of the information on the VRA form if it is incomplete, inconsistent, or unclear, or if the voter is currently registered. If a person currently registered completes the VRA form but indicates a change of name, address, or party affiliation, the change is noted but is not treated as a new registration. Processing in such instances follows standard procedures for changes. If the card contains changes during a period when such changes are not permitted by law—for example, a change of party affiliation during the four months preceding a primary election—the voter is notified of that fact. If the VRA form is received in the local office after the deadline for voter registration prior to an election, the local board is required to notify the prospective registrant that the application cannot be processed until after the election.

The voter is deemed to be registered when he receives his voter-notification form. If the notification form is returned to the election board by the post office as nondeliverable, a second mailing is recommended. In practice, as described below, most offices first attempt to determine by telephone why the form was returned. If the voter-notification form has been returned to the election office but the voter shows up at the polls and is willing to file an affidavit that he or she lives at the address stated on the application and that all other information on the application is correct, the voter will be permitted to vote. Falsification of an affidavit is punishable by law.

Local election boards are required to retain and file all applications, to maintain "suspense" files of applications in process, rejection files, and files of duplicate applications. Rejected applications must be maintained on file for one year and all other applications must be retained for five years or until the boards have separate records of the applicants' signatures.

Court Challenge to the Mail-Registration Law. Within two months of the mail-registration law becoming effective, three residents of Howard County filed a suit in the circuit court attacking the constitutionality of the law and the legality of the rules made by the state board. These voters contended that the law was unconstitutional because it permitted residents of certain counties in Maryland to register by mail while not giving that opportunity to others, thereby denying equal protection of the law. They further asserted that the general rules and regulations of the state board "have not and cannot" prevent fraudulent registrations. The attorney general's office defended the law and its administration, pointing out that the attack on the law was "abstract" and contained no supporting evidence.

In September 1974 the Circuit Court for Howard County ruled that there was no authority which would justify granting the plaintiffs' request that the court declare the law null and void and granted the state's motion for a directed verdict.

Experience with Mail Registration

Baltimore City. No serious voter-registration drives or purges of the rolls had been conducted in Baltimore City for several years prior to 1972. Stories appeared in the press about "ghost voters" and "deadwood" on the books, especially in areas of the city where urban renewal had taken place.[2] Governor Mandel directed the state administrator of election laws to make a comprehensive plan for purging the voter lists throughout the state. The plan was made, but it was implemented only in Baltimore City where it was believed that the greatest numbers of ineligible voters were on the rolls. The purge process required that a nonforwardable first-class mailing be made to every registered voter, and 459,000 postcards were sent. Of the first mailing, 112,800 pieces were reported undeliverable by the post office. Each was followed up with a forwardable first-class letter, and as a result some 15,000 people reported changes of address within the city and were retained on the rolls. More than 92,000 of the letters were still undeliverable and the addressees were purged from the rolls. During approximately the same time period, more than 35,000 new voters were added to the lists, but the net *decline* in the city's voter rolls was over 60,000. This exceptional reduction in the number of registered voters during 1972 reveals the extent to which the Baltimore City lists had become outdated. As a result, total registration figures for the city for the years 1970, 1972, and 1974 are not comparable.

---

[2] Ibid., p. 24.

Baltimore City officials favored mail registration as a means of maintaining voter registration in a city where population mobility was increasing. The city relied heavily on the postcard program to register voters during 1974, and, alone among the jurisdictions in Maryland, provided a *post-paid* self-mailer application. Registration applications were distributed through thirty-one libraries in the city, through community action groups, high schools, department stores, and other locations. Unlike Prince George's county, Baltimore City made its forms widely available.

During the year the city reported receiving 44,769 forms and processing and returning 42,293.[3] Of these, 1,600 were duplicate registrations, 50 were blanks, and 286 contained frivolous information. Nevertheless, the city did register more than 40,000 voters by mail during 1974. This constitutes more than 10 percent of all voters on the registry in Baltimore City.

When voter-registration applications come into the election office in Baltimore, they are immediately checked for duplications and obvious errors, and the appropriate ward, precinct, and election district are determined. Then they are forwarded to data processing. The data processing department makes up all the forms required, including the precinct file and the voter-notification card, and returns them to the board. The voter's name is entered on the rolls and a voter-notification card is sent to him. If the voter-notification card is returned to the local board, then the name of the registered voter is removed from the active precinct file until the proper disposition of the registration can be established. As a result of this procedure, if a voter-notification card is undeliverable but the voter shows up at the polls, his name will be on the rolls unless the election officials have had sufficient time to remove it. This procedure protects voters who register during the final weeks from being denied the right to vote because of postal service error. At the same time, however, persons who do not live at the addresses indicated on the registration forms may be retained on the lists until after the election, at which time the addresses will be checked by second mailings. Baltimore City did not investigate to determine how many, if any, voters whose voter-notification cards had been returned actually showed up at the polls. During the last two weeks prior to the close of the books before the primary election, some 9,000 voters registered by mail in Baltimore.

[3] The total number of registered voters for 1974 was obtained from the city board of elections. This differs somewhat from the total shown in the state report because the state board had not received all the weekly totals from the city prior to publishing the annual report.

Officials managed to process the forms and to send the voter-notification cards, but did not have time to remove from the precinct roster the names of persons whose cards had been returned prior to the election.

Harford County. In Harford County voter-registration forms are distributed through libraries, bookmobiles, town halls, and by candidates and political and civic groups. Harford also responds to individual requests received in writing or on its around-the-clock telephone answering service. Only properly instructed individuals are permitted to distribute the cards to voters. Through the use of coded forms, the performance of the groups was monitored during 1974. As in Montgomery County, there was no evidence that any group was not complying with instructions.

A total of 4,898 voters registered by mail in Harford County in 1974, but an additional 2,744 mail-registration forms were not returned to the office. Approximately 100 duplicates were identified among the 5,000 forms processed.

Officials in Harford County ordinarily waited for one week after mailing a voter-notification card before including the voter in the precinct register. Prior to the election, the lists of voters were placed in the precinct binders and at the same time the voter-notification cards were mailed. No voter's name remained in the book on election day if his voter-notification card had been returned prior to the election. Only two voter-notification cards were returned as undeliverable in Harford County during the entire year.

Harford reported only one difficulty with distribution or processing. One of the candidates, who had distributed approximately ten forms to voters and had collected them himself to return to the board, failed to deliver them before the close of registration. This meant that the applicants were not legally registered to vote. Harford County officials stress the importance of the voter's responsibility to mail or deliver his registration form in person, and point out that the law offers no relief for a voter who loses his opportunity to vote because he fails to do so.

Howard County. During 1974 Howard County distributed 14,162 VRA forms to individuals, institutions, and groups. Although almost 5,000 residents had taken advantage of a twenty-four-hour-a-day telephone-answering service to request VRA forms, only 3,267 actually registered. Another 2,886 persons obtained registration forms from banks and stores (where they were available upon request) and subsequently registered. An additional 1,879 who received forms from political parties or private civic groups were registered. Altogether, 6,993 mail registrations were recorded in the county prior to the 1974 election. This constituted 17 percent of the total voter registration in Howard County in the 1974 general election.

The experience in Howard County indicated that persons who requested voter-registration forms individually, either in person or by telephone, were more likely to register and vote than those who received them as a result of party or group solicitation. Even so, only 68 percent of those who personally requested forms completed and returned them to the local board of elections. Fewer than one-third of the forms distributed by political parties and civic groups were returned to the board.

In Howard County, two file cards are created for each VRA form received by the office, one for the master alpha file and the other for the appropriate polling place. The voter-notification form is then sent to the applicant. Only four voter-notification forms were returned as undeliverable in Howard County in 1974. As required by the state regulations, a second notification was sent to each of the four registrants and when the cards were returned a second time the names were removed from the active files. Howard County reported no polling place challenges and no complaints at the polls from voters who claimed to have registered by mail. This was especially significant in view of the court challenge in Howard County earlier in the year (see page 27).

Howard County maintained a record by precinct of mail voter registration and subsequent voter turnout in the general election of 1974. There are 35 precincts in the county, with an average voter registration of 1,187 per precinct and some precincts having over 2,000 registered voters. For the county as a whole, 67 percent of all persons who registered by mail voted in the 1974 general election. Most precincts were very near the average, although in one small precinct— District 1, Precinct 3—only 48 percent of mail registrants voted. The highest proportion of mail registrants voting in any precinct was 80 percent (see Table 14).

Personal voter registration took place in the county office building and at public locations during the year. The Howard County election office is open on Tuesdays, Wednesdays, and Thursdays from 8:30 to 12:00 noon, and from 1:00 to 4:30 p.m. It is closed on Mondays, Fridays, and weekends.

Montgomery County. Montgomery County distributed its VRA forms through election officials, at unstaffed locations, and through cooperating groups, but in each instance county authorities exercised substantial control over the process in an attempt to avoid frivolous distribution and erroneous applications. Election officials distributed the VRA forms to persons who came into the election office to register, sent them by mail to persons who had made requests in writing or by telephone, and made the forms available on Thursday evenings at five shopping centers staffed by election office employees. Use of the mail-registration forms in the office or at the field sites made it possible for each election office employee to process several applications in the time that had previously been needed for two registrars, one from each party, to register a single person. Table 5 shows the number of persons who registered each month with election officials, either in the county office or at a field site. Montgomery County also provides a twenty-four-hour-a-day telephone information service which

Table 5

NEW VOTER REGISTRATION IN MONTGOMERY COUNTY,
BY MONTH, 1974

Month	Registrations Received by Mail	Registrations Received in Office or Field Sites	Total
January	1,171	324	1,495
February	1,236	176	1,412
March	1,355	286	1,641
April	1,071	280	1,351
May	886	260	3,520[a]
June	1,078	323	1,401
July	2,359	335	2,694
August[b]	3,085	3,507	6,592
September–October[c]	4,302	3,513	7,815
November	729	44	773
December	289	97	386
Total	17,561	9,145	29,079[a]

[a] Includes 2,374 registered in annual high school drive.
[b] 1 to 12 August only. Registry closed 13 August through 22 September for primary election.
[c] Registry open only 23 September through 7 October between primary and general election; reopened 21 November after the general election.
Source: Montgomery County Board of Supervisors of Elections.

plays a recorded message about voter registration and permits the caller to record his request for a VRA form.

During 1974 Montgomery County also made the VRA form available at all public libraries in the county, but did not have the forms in view. Librarians posted signs informing readers that voter-registration applications were available upon request. This procedure was adopted to prevent anyone from taking large numbers of forms for unauthorized use.

Students in the county high schools were made deputy registrars and, after training, were permitted to distribute cards to their classmates. This procedure produced 2,374 registrations during 1974. In the nonelection year of 1975, when the effort was aided by the vigorous promotion of the Board of Education, more than 6,000 young people were registered.

More than 500 persons, including many from political and civic groups, completed a one-and-a-half hour training program and were authorized to distribute VRA forms during 1975. These groups included representatives of the major political parties, the League of Women Voters, labor organizations, community action groups, teachers' associations, and retired persons. Several precinct chairmen also completed the training program in order to be able to promote voter registration in their own precincts. During the training session, prospective distributors of registration forms were cautioned against improper use of the cards, and the fact that the voter was responsible for the return of his own application, in person or by mail, was emphasized. Distributors were also advised that the success of the mail-registration program depended upon their compliance with the law and that unless they did their job well, the state legislature might return to the old system of personal voter registration.

Instructions were followed so completely that no group was even warned about the quality of its work. Mail registrations were complete, legible, and, according to veteran registration officials, much easier to work with than those filled out by paid registrars under the old system.

Voter registration in Montgomery County has been the highest in the state, about 90 percent of the voting-age population (according to estimates of the state board). During 1974 the county registered 29,079 voters, 60 percent of them by mail.[4] The remainder used the

---

[4] The total number of registered voters for 1974 was obtained from the Montgomery County Board of Elections. This figure, too, differs from that cited in the state report because certain registration information was not available to the state at the time the annual report was completed.

mail-registration form but actually registered in person at various locations staffed by registrars throughout the county. More than 5,000 persons under the age of twenty-one were included in the 1974 registrations in Montgomery County.

Prince George's County. Prince George's County differed from the other Maryland jurisdictions considered here in the manner by which it distributed voter-registration forms. In Prince George's County voter forms were sent *only* to the individual voter and distributed *only* through the county election office.

Rather than permit widespread distribution of the voter-registration form itself, county officials devised a registration application which was widely disseminated by individuals and groups (see below). Applications could be returned in batches by groups to the board of elections, which would then send voter-registration cards to the individuals requesting them. A twenty-four-hour-a-day telephone-answering service was also installed, and the policy was that any county resident who requested a registration card by phone would receive it in the mail the next day. No training of registration form distributors was necessary because no individuals or groups distributed the actual voter-registration card. Applications by prospective registrants were, nevertheless, very legible, complete, and accurate, and little clarification was required. Prince George's County was the only jurisdiction to request the social security number of prospective registrants. This was not actually required for voter registration by state law, and failure to include it did not prevent processing of the form nor affect the eligibility of the registrant to vote.

Prince George's County also differed from the other Maryland counties in that it registered substantial numbers of voters by the traditional method. Of 25,503 voters registered during 1974, 14,485 were registered by mail. Another 11,018 were registered in person at shopping centers, schools, other public locations, and in the county office, using the two-registrar method and the standard voter-registration forms. Voters registered in the latter manner were given their voter-notification cards at the time of registration. Those who registered early in the year, however, received the mailings sent out by the county to all registered voters, and all voters on the rolls as of 1 August 1974 received at least one general mailing from the county election board.

Voter registration has traditionally been lower in Prince George's County than in most Maryland jurisdictions. This is generally attrib-

Figure 1

Application for Voter Registration
Prince George's County, Maryland
(PLEASE PRINT OR TYPE)

NAME _____
FIRST   MIDDLE   LAST   (Jr., Sr., Etc.)   TELEPHONE

RESIDENCE ADDRESS _____
If P.O. Box is used it is necessary to list residence address or nearest road.   APT. NO.

_____, Maryland _____
POST OFFICE   ZIP

PLEASE CHECK   PLACE OF BIRTH _____ DATE OF BIRTH _____
☐ Male   ☐ Female   STATE OR COUNTRY   MONTH-DAY-YEAR
☐ Civilian   ☐ Military

_____   _____
SOCIAL SECURITY NUMBER   PRESENT AGE

PARTY AFFILIATION

I wish to affiliate with a political party (check one).

DEMOCRAT ☐

REPUBLICAN ☐

DECLINE ☐
(I do not wish to affiliate with a political party.)

OTHER (Specify) _____

I am a citizen of the United States and a resident of Prince George's County, Maryland. I have not been convicted of a disqualifying crime. I am not under guardianship for mental disability.

I do solemnly swear (or affirm) that the information set forth hereon about my place of residence, name, place of birth, criminal offenses, qualifications as a voter and my right to register and vote under the laws of this State is true.

X _____
SIGNATURE

GIVING FALSE INFORMATION TO PROCURE VOTER REGISTRATION IS PERJURY AND IS PUNISHABLE BY IMPRISONMENT FOR NOT MORE THAN TEN YEARS.

HAVE YOU REGISTERED TO VOTE BEFORE? ☐ YES ☐ NO

(If YES—Complete This Form)

Please Print or Type

NAME ON LAST REGISTRATION _____
FIRST   MIDDLE   LAST   (JR., SR., ETC.)

ADDRESS ON LAST REGISTRATION _____
STREET

_____
CITY/COUNTY   STATE   ZIP

Party Affiliation On Last Registration _____
DATE OF BIRTH

I am aware that a change of party affiliation within four months of any primary election is prohibited by law and I declare that my decision to cancel my registration is not related in any way to an effort on my part to change my party affiliation at a time when such action is not permitted.

_____   X _____
Date   Signature of Voter

Note: The top third of the application form, omitted here, contains instructions for filling out the form.

Source: Board of Supervisors of Elections for Prince George's County, Maryland, Prince George's Form 723-M, January 1974.

uted to four factors. Prince George's population is high in character-istics usually associated with low registration and voting. These include race and age factors and the transiency of the population, as well as the presence of large military and educational institutions. Further, the county's registration books are systematically purged every year to remove the names of persons who have not voted for five years. In addition, special mailings have resulted in the removal of names of persons who have moved. The frequency of Prince George's mailings to all registered voters and the subsequent adjustments have kept the county's registration lists accurate and current throughout the year as well as at election time.

A special mailing was conducted in the spring of 1974 which resulted in the removal of 34,227 registered voters, or 14.6 percent of the total registration in the county. This mailing was for the purpose of obtaining social security numbers for identification and was a first-class nonforwardable communication. When the request letters were returned to the election office by the postal service as undeliverable, a forwardable "Form B" was sent out. This form contained the following message:

> After a recent mailing the United States Postal Service has informed us that you no longer reside at the address indicated on this notice. Please provide us with your proper address, in writing, within two weeks from the above date. If not received, we will assume you have moved and your name will be removed from the registration rolls.

Again in August a mailing was sent to every registered voter notifying him of the location of the precinct polling place for the September primary election. Of the 203,292 cards sent, 5,236 were returned as undeliverable, even though the addresses had come from a list that had been totally purged only a few months before. Ultimately, some 926 of the August returns resulted in corrected addresses or changes of address, but 4,240 of the names were removed from the registry early in 1975. These figures illustrate quite clearly the mobility of the population in Prince George's County and help to explain why that county has a lower registration as a proportion of voting-age population than any other county in the state.

Table 6 lists the total registration for Prince George's County, by month, during 1974. Even though the county actually registered some 25,503 new voters, that is, about 12 percent of the total registration, the net effect for the entire year in which postcard registration was available was a decline in total registration of 24,835.

Table 6

TOTAL VOTER REGISTRATION IN PRINCE GEORGE'S COUNTY, BY MONTH, 1974

Month	Total Voter Registration	Gain or Loss from Previous Month
January	239,974	—
February	229,513	− 10,461
March	231,723	+ 2,210
April	234,126	− 2,403
May	235,698	− 1,572
June	201,897	− 33,801
July	203,519	+ 1,621
August	209,660	+ 6,142
September	208,883	− 777
October	215,139	+ 7,256
Net loss for year at close of registration		− 24,835

Source: Registration figures from Prince George's County Board of Supervisors of Elections.

Reactions of Maryland Officials to Mail Registration.[5] Election officials in the counties that implemented voter registration by mail in 1974 were enthusiastic about the way in which the system had operated. At a meeting held in Annapolis in January 1975, each reported that by controlling the distribution of the mail-registration form, instructing those who were to distribute the form, and auditing the results of group distribution by coding each form with a number, the administrative problems that had been anticipated were minimized. No major problems had affected the administration of the mail-registration system. While their assessments of the system's effectiveness in registering new voters varied, all officials agreed that mail registration was far simpler than the traditional system which required a Democratic and a Republican registrar to complete the forms for each applicant.

With the exception of Baltimore City, the Maryland jurisdictions that use mail registration have been growing rapidly and the number

---

[5] The data in this section are based upon author interviews with county officials and oral reports made by election officials from mail-registration counties at a 29 January 1975 meeting in Annapolis called by the state board of elections.

of persons eligible to register each election year is a significant proportion of the population. Maryland only conducts elections every two years and almost all new registration takes place in the election year. Officials from all jurisdictions reported that mail registration helped reduce the number of last-minute registrations, thereby easing the workload on their offices and eliminating long lines for the voters. Table 7 compares the number of 1974 registrations in each mail-registration jurisdiction and the total registration on the books as of election day 1974.

Maryland state and local election officials also voiced strong support for legislation which would implement voter registration by mail on a statewide basis. By that time mail registration had already been authorized in Baltimore and Anne Arundel counties, the two largest counties which had not used the system in 1974. Two factors were responsible for the change of attitude between 1974, when most officials opposed the concept, and 1975, when almost all favored the system: first, the favorable experience of the counties which had implemented mail registration and, second, the likelihood that a federal mail-registration system would be enacted. Maryland officials, with few exceptions, strongly oppose federal involvement in voter registration in general and a federal mail-registration system in particular. Many present at the Annapolis meeting expressed hope that the adoption of mail registration by the state might exempt Maryland from the provisions of national legislation.

Table 7

NEW VOTER REGISTRATION AND TOTAL VOTER REGISTRATION IN MARYLAND COUNTIES WITH MAIL REGISTRATION, 1974

County	Total Registration	1974 Registration	Percent Registered in 1974
Baltimore City	389,596	42,293	11
Harford	51,197	5,135	10
Howard	41,546	6,993	17
Montgomery	291,280	29,079	10
Prince George's	215,139	25,503	12

Source: Registration figures from boards of supervisors of elections of the five jurisdictions.

Most Maryland officials believe that the success of their system has been due to the controlled distribution of voter-registration cards. They think that uncontrolled distribution of registration forms by a federal agency would lead to many problems, including duplicate registrations, illegible applications, and an increase in voter fraud and malicious mischief. Maryland officials oppose a dual registration system, which could result if federal legislation were passed and the state refused to accept the federal registration form for voting in state elections. A federal mail-registration system would have no advantages and great disadvantages, according to Maryland officials.

3
MAIL REGISTRATION IN NEW JERSEY

New Jersey is the eighth most populous state in the nation, but the fifth smallest in land area. With 953 people per square mile, it is the country's most densely populated state. During the 1960s, New Jersey's population increased by 18 percent, brought about partly by a net migration growth of 488,000 people, second only to that of California.[1] The state has a black population of about 11 percent which is concentrated in the northeastern counties of Hudson, Essex, and Union. Selected population characteristics of New Jersey counties are presented in Table 8.

The twenty-one counties of New Jersey are the basic units of government responsible for voter registration. In addition, the state has 536 municipalities, school districts, and special-purpose districts which exercise governmental powers and conduct elections. All elections are conducted in accordance with the provisions of the New Jersey Election Code. Voters may register either with the county or with the municipality in order to be eligible to vote in all elections held within the jurisdiction in which they reside.

New Jersey's Election Laws

A uniform system of election laws governs all municipal, county, state, and federal elections held in New Jersey, but its application varies somewhat from place to place. There are variations in the law, for example, according to the size or "class" of the jurisdiction. Also, New Jersey's election administration is much more decentralized than that of Maryland, and divides responsibility at the county and mu-

---

[1] Neal R. Peirce, *The Megastates of America* (New York: Norton, 1972), p. 184. The politics of New Jersey is described in Chapter 3, pp. 181-226.

Table 8

POPULATION CHARACTERISTICS OF NEW JERSEY COUNTIES, 1970

	Race (in thousands)		Percent Negro	Percent Spanish Origin	Median Annual Family Income ($)	Median Education (years completed)	Percent Completed Four Years of College	Percent Owner-Occupied Housing Units
	White	Negro						
Atlantic	144	30	17.2	1.5	8,767	11.2	6.2	62.2
Bergen	868	25	2.8	.4	13,591	12.3	15.6	67.7
Burlington	293	28	8.7	.8	11,352	12.3	12.6	72.5
Camden	403	52	11.4	1.6	10,959	11.9	9.8	71.7
Cape May	54	4	6.9		8,295	11.3	7.3	77.4
Cumberland	103	16	13.4	4.5	9,522	10.7	5.7	68.3
Essex	644	279	30.2	3.1	10,682	11.9	12.2	40.6
Gloucester	157	14	8.2	.6	10,620	11.8	8.0	77.6
Hudson	543	61	39.9	5.3	9,695	10.2	5.6	29.6
Hunterdon	68	1	1.4		11,336	12.2	12.1	74.3
Mercer	252	50	16.5	1.1	11,165	12.1	14.1	65.3
Middlesex	556	26	4.4	1.9	11,981	12.1	11.2	69.2
Monmouth	419	38	8.3	.8	11,632	12.3	14.3	69.8
Morris	373	8	2.1	.7	13,420	12.5	19.9	73.0
Ocean	201	6	2.9	1.2	9,245	11.9	7.3	80.1
Passaic	408	49	10.7	4.3	10,917	11.1	8.4	53.1
Salem	50	9	15.2		10,214	11.3	5.7	71.1
Somerset	190	7	3.5	.4	13,432	12.4	19.0	73.1
Sussex	77				10,785	12.2	9.8	78.0
Union	480	61	11.3	.9	12,590	12.2	14.0	63.3
Warren	74	1	1.4	.9	10,117	11.8	7.2	69.5
NEW JERSEY	6,362	769	9.8	1.9	11,403	12.1	11.8	60.9

Source: U.S. Bureau of the Census, *County and City Data Book, 1972* (Washington, D. C.: Government Printing Office, 1973).

nicipal levels. The secretary of state, superintendent of elections, county boards of elections, commissioners of registration, and county and municipal clerks all have statutory and discretionary authority in implementing the law. Further, decisions regarding voter registration may be appealed and decided in court on election day.

Election schedule. A voter in New Jersey has the opportunity to go to the polls no fewer than twice and sometimes four or more times each year. A partisan primary election is conducted every June and a general election every November. Federal elections are held during even-numbered years. State elections for members of the General Assembly are conducted every two years in odd-numbered years and the governor is elected for a four-year term in odd-numbered years. The most recent gubernatorial election was in 1973. Municipalities which conduct nonpartisan primary elections hold them in May, and school board elections are held in February. Special district elections and other special elections can be held at times other than those specified above.

Election districts. New Jersey's smallest administrative unit for the conduct of elections is known as an "election district" rather than a "precinct," the term employed in most states. Election districts are intentionally small. Small districts are not only more convenient for voters and for political party officials during election campaigns, but also increase the likelihood that election district judges will recognize voters and hence protect against voter fraud. Table 9 compares the average voter registration for election districts in New Jersey with that for precincts in Maryland.

Voter-registration requirements. Any citizen of the United States eighteen years of age or older who has resided in New Jersey for thirty days preceding a general election and who is a resident of a county and of a municipality is eligible to register at any time. Persons who register during a twenty-eight-day period prior to any election are not eligible to vote in the immediate election but may vote in all subsequent elections. Persons who will be eighteen years of age by the time of the general election are permitted to register but are not permitted to vote in any election which occurs before they are eighteen years of age. Persons convicted of certain crimes, including misdemeanors which are violations of election law, are disfranchised until pardoned or restored by law to the right of suffrage.

Once registered in New Jersey, a voter remains registered until he or she dies, moves out of the county, changes his name, is disfranchised for committing a crime, or is judged to be of unsound mind.

Table 9

NUMBER OF REGISTERED VOTERS PER ELECTION DISTRICT IN NEW JERSEY AND PER PRECINCT IN MARYLAND

New Jersey			Maryland		
Counties	Number of Election Districts	Average Voter Regis-tration	Counties	Number of Precincts	Average Voter Regis-tration
Atlantic	165	572	Allegany	68	595
Bergen	544	885	Anne Arundel	82	1,526
Burlington	264	511	Baltimore City	548	710
Camden	354	646	Baltimore County	271	1,121
Cape May	75	550	Calvert	10	946
Cumberland	111	499	Caroline	9	857
Essex	600	650	Carroll	23	1,190
Gloucester	182	479	Cecil	13	1,549
Hudson	404	668	Charles	13	1,633
Hunterdon	63	555	Dorchester	24	533
Mercer	267	602	Frederick	32	1,163
Middlesex	468	603	Garrett	20	505
Monmouth	365	618	Harford	25	2,047
Morris	310	610	Howard	35	1,187
Ocean	179	788	Kent	11	745
Passaic	249	796	Montgomery	142	2,051
Salem	72	429	Prince George's	138	1,558
Somerset	182	552	Queen Anne's	10	849
Sussex	73	558	St. Mary's	9	1,883
Union	455	609	Somerset	19	519
Warren	79	442	Talbot	15	761
NEW JERSEY	5,461	641	Washington	45	963
			Wicomico	23	1,060
			Worcester	8	1,347
			MARYLAND	1,593	1,091

Source: Elections Section, New Jersey Department of State and Maryland State Administrative Board of Election Laws.

Voters are also removed from the registry for failure to vote in at least one general election in a four-year period.

Persons who move out of an election district during the twenty-eight-day period in which they are not able to register at the new address are permitted by law to vote at the former address provided they sign an affidavit. This process, in effect, constitutes a change-of-address notification to the commissioner of registration.

Election Administration

The Secretary of State. The secretary of state of New Jersey is appointed by the governor. Prior to the enactment of mail voter registration, the secretary had only limited duties in the area of voter registration and elections. These consisted of ministerial functions pertaining to candidate certification, recording and publishing the results of elections, and similar nondiscretionary duties. New Jersey has an Election Law Enforcement Commission which, as an independent agency, is charged with enforcing campaign finance and personal disclosure laws but not voter-registration laws. The office of secretary of state has become a controversial position in New Jersey because the last three incumbents have left office after indictments prior to the completion of their terms. The most recent was J. Edward Crabiel, appointed by Governor Byrne, who is now on leave after indictment for extortion. In each instance, the secretary was charged for acts which occurred before he took office as secretary of state.

The current election law gives the secretary of state broad powers to promulgate rules and regulations pursuant to law, "all of which shall have the force of law." The secretary is charged with preparing registration forms and providing them to the commissioners of registration. The secretary is obliged to reimburse the counties at a rate of fifty cents per new registrant, regardless of whether the registration was by mail or in person, and to pay an additional twelve cents if the registration was returned by mail using the county mailing permit number. In addition, the secretary must approve the evening and mobile voter-registration plans submitted by each county and ensure that serious voter-registration drives are conducted, especially in the peak registration periods. These duties are carried out under the direction of the assistant secretary of state, whose office is located in the state capitol and is staffed with four persons.

County Election Officials. Each county has a board of elections consisting of four members, two from each of the two major political parties in the state. Larger counties are permitted by law to appoint a clerk to the board. Appointments to the county boards are made by the governor, but the nominations are made by a committee consisting of the "chairman and vice-chairlady" of each county committee and the state committeeman and state committeewoman of each of the two major political parties. In counties which have a superintendent of elections, the county board plays a passive role. The county board of elections is traditionally considered a political body, and responsibility for its functions is vested in the superintendent of elections, where there is one, and the commissioner of registration. The superintendent of elections is the principal election officer of New Jersey counties of the first class. The superintendent is named by the governor with the advice and consent of the Senate for a term of five years from the date of appointment until a successor has been appointed and qualified. The superintendent has the power to enforce the election law, including the investigation of all complaints relating to the registration of voters. This power covers inspection of dwellings, including motels, hotels, and rooming houses, to determine whether persons listed as registered voters actually reside where they claim to live. The superintendent has subpoena power and may compel persons to testify under oath. The law goes so far as to specify that the superintendent may require landlords of temporary dwellings to provide physical descriptions, including color, height, weight, age, nationality, occupation, and place of business, together with the dates of residence, of all persons who rent or lease premises. The superintendent is also charged with purging the books.

There is, in addition, a commissioner of registration in each county. In any county which provides for a superintendent of elections, that officer also serves as commissioner of registration. Otherwise, the county board designates its secretary or clerk to serve as commissioner. The commissioner of registration prepares and executes the registration plan for the county and is responsible for maintaining the registration lists and removing persons who become ineligible to vote due to death, disfranchisement, or moving from the county. This official has considerable flexibility in the exercise of these functions, but, under the new law, must submit certain plans to the secretary of state and must maintain the registration hours provided by law.

Finally, county and municipal clerks provide certain services in connection with elections. The county clerk has no direct responsibility for voter registration, but he is required by law to make the list of registered voters available, in handbill form, to any voter at the rate of twenty-five cents per election district. (If electronic data or tape is used, the charge must be limited to the cost of duplication.) The clerk also provides five copies to the district board and is responsible for posting the list in the polling place and in one other conspicuous place within the election district. Other copies must be delivered to the municipal clerks and the county board, and five copies of each district list must be delivered to the chairmen of the county committees of the political parties. The county clerk is also responsible for printing ballots, including absentee ballots, and for mailing the ballots to qualified absentee voters. Absentee ballots are returned to the county board of elections. The county clerk is also required to prepare sample ballots for mailing to every registered voter prior to every primary and general election. Municipal clerks provide similar services for municipal elections and often cooperate with county clerks in the fulfillment of their responsibilities. In addition, county and municipal clerks may serve as deputy registrars.

Voter Registration. New Jersey law spells out the details of the voter-registration process more completely than does the law of any other state. Mail registration is encouraged. Door-to-door registration is *required* by law in presidential election years and authorized in other years. The law requires the commissioner of registration of each county to file registration plans prior to the primary and the general election. These plans must provide for evening registration between 4 p.m. and 9 p.m. on at least six working days immediately preceding the close of registration, and at least once a week between 6 p.m. and 9 p.m. during the six weeks immediately prior to the close of registration. The plans must also include arrangements for mobile registration in each municipality with a population of more than 7,500 and must cover the types of vehicle to be used, schedules, and routes. Registration officials must visit every public and nonpublic high school, and school officials are required to cooperate with the commissioners of registration. Each county is required to publish the schedule for voter registration in the newspapers.

The law requires the commissioners of registration to remove from the permanent registry the names of all persons known to have died or moved out of the permanent registration area, or to have been disqualified or improperly registered. Willful failure to purge the rolls is a misdemeanor.

New Jersey residents, with the exception of members of the armed services and a small and specified class of civilians, were required to register in person prior to the passage of the law authorizing voter registration by mail. To register in person, New Jersey residents must appear before properly authorized registration officials and must provide the basic information required by law. Registration officials include municipal and county clerks as well as employees of the county boards of elections. Registration is conducted at all county court houses and at various locations throughout the county as determined by the commissioner of registration. Evening hours other than those specified by law may be scheduled.

Voter Identification at the Polling Place. Proper identification of the voter at the polling place is extremely important in New Jersey because so little information is required on the registration form. The state relies heavily on signature comparisons to determine whether the person who offers to vote is, in fact, the person who is registered. The first time a registered voter comes to the polls, he is required to sign the duplicate permanent registration form at the polls in the space provided for a sample signature. Every subsequent time he votes, the voter is required to sign this same form in the box designated for the current election and calendar year. In practice, in New Jersey and in other states, few voters are challenged on the basis of dissimilar signatures. The form is shown below.

Voters whose names do not appear on the books at the polling place may seek relief from administrative officials or through the courts by establishing that they are qualified to vote and that their names have been omitted from the registry through no fault of their own. Election judges are also permitted to challenge persons whose names are on the lists of registered voters but whose eligibility is questionable. For example, if a voter registers by mail but his voter-notification form is returned by the postal service and the voter appears at the polling place, he may be challenged. Only if the voter can satisfy the election district officials that the residence is correct will voting be permitted. If not, a court order will be required before the voter is permitted to vote.

Purges of Voter-Registration Lists. New Jersey law provides for systematic notification to commissioners of registration of deaths and conviction for crimes. The commissioner of registration, after ascertaining that a registered voter has died, been convicted of a disqualifying crime, never resided at the address indicated, or moved from the address indicated on the registration form, may order that the person's name may be removed from the rolls. The commissioner must give notice to the registrant, however, and must publish the names of persons affected by such action. Persons whose names are removed by administrative action may seek relief in the county court up to and including the day of election. If the judge is satisfied that any applicant is entitled to vote, he may issue an order to the election district board directing them to permit the applicant to vote regardless of previous administrative decisions.

Many revisions of the registry result from returns of the sample ballots which are mailed to every registered voter in June and in November. A voter whose sample ballot is returned as undeliverable

Figure 2

FORM FOR NEW JERSEY POLLING PLACE SIGNATURE COMPARISON RECORD

YEAR	SAMPLE SIGNATURE					
	SIG. COMP. BY	PRIMARY	SIG. COMP. BY	GENERAL	SIG. COMP. BY	ANY OTHER ELECTIONS
1941						
1942						
1943						
1944						
1945						
1946						
1947						
1948						
1949						
1950						
1951						
1952						

Source: New Jersey Election Code, section 19.31A-7, as revised January 1973, p. 126.

is notified that he must confirm the residence address on the record, provide a new current residence address, or be removed from the list of registered voters. In practice, these names are not removed from the list before the immediate election because of lack of time. Further, the law protects the right to vote of persons who move to new addresses during the period immediately preceding an election. Following the election, however, most counties routinely remove all voters who are presumed to have moved.

Procedures for Voter Registration by Mail [2]

The mail-registration law supported by Governor Brendan Byrne was passed by the legislature in May 1974 and became effective on 28 August, approximately seven weeks prior to the close of registration before the 1974 general election.

Rules. The 1971 law provided the secretary of state with discretionary authority to develop rules and regulations to implement mail registration. This was accomplished in cooperation with the commissioners of registration. A seminar was held in August to instruct registration officials in the new procedures.

In general, the rules and regulations adopted are designed to make registration as easy as possible.[3] The form itself is very brief. It does not require the applicant to state sex or marital status. Moreover, it asks no questions about either conviction for crimes or mental incompetence even though the laws of New Jersey withhold the franchise from certain classes of persons for those reasons. No voter is denied registration for failure to complete the form if the information left out is age, previous residence, county of residence, zip code—or, when the applicant is a naturalized citizen, the date, municipality, and state of naturalization. Information not submitted on the registration form may be requested at the polling place.

The rules also provide that each voter must be notified immediately after his registration has been accepted or rejected. The voter-notification process is similar to that used in Maryland. The

---

[2] In addition to the sources cited, the data in this and the next section are based upon author interviews with New Jersey county and state officials. At least one election official was interviewed in every county, and in some more than one official was interviewed or follow-up interviews were conducted. Interviews were also held with the assistant secretary of state, with the administrator in charge of mail registration in the Elections Section of the Department of State, and with some county and municipal clerks.

[3] *New Jersey Register*, Thursday, 5 September 1974, p. 16 (6 N.J.R. 356).

New Jersey form requests the postal service to return any voter notification not delivered in two days.

Distribution of Forms. The rules facilitate wide distribution of registration forms. Organizations, political parties, and candidates for public office are permitted to obtain a "reasonable" number of forms upon request, and the number of requests allowed is unlimited. Photocopies and newspaper reproductions of the form were ruled acceptable. The commissioners of registration were authorized to number the forms if they wished to do so, but were prohibited from rejecting forms which were not numbered, which were facsimiles, or which originated in other areas of the state. On 28 August, the first day of mail voter registration, the *Times-Advertiser* of Pemberton, in Burlington County, and other newspapers in the state printed reproductions of the mail-registration form. Attempts to control distribution of the forms by the commissioners of registration were quickly abandoned.

To the extent that political parties and organized groups distributed registration forms, the New Jersey mail-registration system approximated an unpaid deputy-registrar system. In the more populous counties of Bergen, Essex, and Mercer, groups hand-delivered between 55 percent and 85 percent of all registration forms processed after the law went into effect. In less populous counties, such as Ocean County, more than half the forms were returned by mail.

The quality and manner of distribution of registration forms by political groups varied greatly. Officials reported that some canvassed carefully and attempted to register only unregistered voters, whereas others distributed the forms door-to-door, like political handouts. This was neither illegal nor improper. Some enthusiastic partisans, however, signed the forms as "witnesses" to registrations before actually distributing them. This practice came to light when the commissioner of registration received registration forms on which the signatures of witness and registrant were dated on different days. Some commissioners gave the registrants the benefit of the doubt and proceeded to register them, but others did not. Group distributors also turned in some registration forms on which the registrants had signed only their initials rather than their full names. Again, some commissioners accepted these forms and others rejected them.

In Monmouth County, the commissioner of registration rejected 409 mail registrations out of a total of 5,360 submitted. These were rejected because there was a discrepancy between the date of the registrant's signature and the date of the witness's signature, because the signature of the registrant was incorrect or incomplete, or because the witness had not signed the form or was not a registered voter. These reasons were all in accordance with the rules, but few commissioners adhered this strictly to the letter of the law. On election day, six voters whose registration forms had been rejected appeared in court seeking court orders permitting them to vote. The public advocate, who serves as an ombudsman representing the public in seeking rights apparently denied by government agencies, represented the voters. The attorney general's office defended the commissioner of registration, but the judge, ruling on each case individually, determined that each of the six persons was qualified to vote and should be permitted to do so, technical deficiencies in the registration form notwithstanding. As a result of that decision, the commissioner of elections, of her own volition, placed the names of the remaining 403 persons on the registration rolls. She reasoned that, had they been in court, they would have been awarded similar decisions.[4]

County offices responded in different ways to the requirement that they verify the signature of the witness on a mail-registration form. In practice the witness's signature was verified when the time and staff were available and when the witness was registered to vote in the county. When the witness was from outside the county, offices with sufficient staff sometimes checked his registration by telephone or by letter, a cumbersome process, but only one county in the state reported that no voter was registered until the witness's signature had been verified. Most officials took the position that their job was to ensure the operation of the system rather than to insist on rigid application of the rules at every step. One county official reported that his county conducted a random check of every 150th application processed. Many election officials were of the opinion that voter-registration check was much less important than the verification of the voter's signature at the polls. Some thought that the signature of the witness was superfluous because "it didn't prove anything."

Counties also seemed to respond somewhat differently when the postal service returned a voter-notification form. All reported that the first step was to check for possible error by the registration office. Some immediately pulled the registration card and placed it in an inactive file until further information could be obtained. Some counties reported sending an investigator to the address indicated to verify the registration. Others admitted frankly that if the election was near,

---

[4] Superintendent of Elections and Commissioner of Registration C. Nancy Crowell, from Monmouth County, N.J., and Assistant Secretary of State F. Joseph Carragher provided information about this court case.

they took no steps other than to call the attention of the polling place officials to the situation so that accurate information could be obtained if the voter appeared at the polls. If the commissioner of registration had good working relationships with the tax officials or municipal clerks who might have information about potential registered voters, these officials were sometimes contacted. In brief, the election officials in New Jersey worked pragmatically, usually assuming the good faith of the voter but checking each registration to the extent that time and circumstances permitted. As a last resort, they left the decision about the status of the voter to the officials at the polling place.

The rules provide that registration forms signed by the registrant on or before the close of registration "shall be deemed timely" if received no later than seven days after the close of registration. This rule had the effect of reducing by one week the time available for processing the registrations prior to the election. There were complaints by some officials that political parties or groups brought in "piles of forms" after the close of registration, but because the forms had been signed and dated prior to the deadline, they had to be accepted. Not all the registration forms delivered near or after the deadline were checked to verify the signature of the witness, nor was there sufficient time in all instances for the mailing and possible return of the voter-notification card. The effect of "extending the deadline" by this rule varied according to the size of the county. Few smaller counties needed the full thirty days to prepare for an election, but the larger counties were burdened by this extra pressure at a critical time.

Experience with Mail Registration

Results. It is very difficult to evaluate the New Jersey mail-registration program on the basis of the data available. Unlike the Maryland counties, most New Jersey counties did not keep detailed records of the number of forms that were duplicates, merely address changes, or unacceptable because they were illegible or incomplete or of the number of voter-notification cards returned by the post office. Some counties included in the total number of mail registrations persons who merely reported changes of address by using the mail-registration form. Some "reregistered" persons by mail whose names and correct addresses were already on the lists, which extended the voters' protection against removal for nonvoting to four years from the date of the mail registration. This practice maintains the voting eligibility of registrants without compromising the integrity of the system, but it also produces some overreporting of *new* registrants. New Jersey reported more than 135,000 new registrants prior to the November election, 78,935 of whom registered by mail. Given the way in which mail registrations were processed, it is not possible to determine exactly how many of these were, in fact, *new* registrations. (See Table 10 for a county-by-county report of 1974 mail registrations.)

The number of voters newly recorded on the registration lists in New Jersey constituted 3.9 percent of the total number of voters eligible to vote in 1974. This figure ranged from a high of 7.6 percent

Table 10

NEW VOTER REGISTRATION AS A PERCENT OF TOTAL REGISTRATION, NEW JERSEY COUNTIES, 1974

County	Total Registration	1974 Registration		Percent Registered in 1974
		Mail	Total	
Atlantic	94,493	2,104	4,824	5.1
Bergen	481,290	5,356	11,811	2.4
Burlington	134,973	4,835	7,772	5.7
Camden	228,748	11,776	17,888	7.8
Cape May	41,254	434	1,720	4.2
Cumberland	55,376	1,450	2,107	3.8
Essex	390,167	3,359	6,217	1.6
Gloucester	87,191	3,420	5,035	5.8
Hudson	270,110	7,075	9,030	3.3
Hunterdon	34,945	486	1,225	3.5
Mercer	160,810	4,098	6,142	3.8
Middlesex	282,819	5,698	12,975	4.6
Monmouth	225,786	5,360	9,398	4.2
Morris	189,478	2,930	8,289	4.4
Ocean	141,676	6,981	9,825	6.9
Passaic	198,537	1,593	3,426	1.7
Salem	30,943	1,652	1,652	5.3
Somerset	100,498	3,196	4,672	4.6
Sussex	40,770	1,068	2,392	5.9
Union	277,341	4,644	7,439	2.7
Warren	34,970	420	1,096	3.1
NEW JERSEY	3,502,175	78,935	135,935	3.9

Source: Elections Section, New Jersey Department of State.

in Camden County to a low of 1.6 percent in Essex County. As expected, the counties with the highest growth rates generally recorded the highest percentages of new voters. These included Ocean, Atlantic, Gloucester, and Sussex counties, each of which had more than 5 percent of' its total registration newly registered in 1974 (see Table 10).

The total number of registered voters was 39,000 fewer in 1974 than it had been in 1973 for the gubernatorial election. This pattern appears to be consistent with New Jersey registration and voting history. It may be too early to determine whether mail registration can increase voter registration in New Jersey. State officials report that the increase between the primary election and the general election was larger than for comparable periods, even though mail registration did not become effective in New Jersey until August, *after* the 1974 primary election. Nevertheless, it is difficult to determine how many of the mail registrations reported were new registrations, and until this can be done, any conclusion that mail registration has increased voter registration will be premature.

Turning to the impact on voter turnout, it appears very doubtful that merely increasing the number of registered voters increases the number who vote. There were 335,000 more registered voters in 1974 than in 1970, but the actual turnout in 1974 was 26,000 less, and the percentage of registered voters voting decreased seven points. Another comparison is that between the gubernatorial election of 1973 and the congressional election of 1974. In this instance, voter turnout as a percentage of registered voters voting increased by one percentage point, from 61 percent of registered voters to 62 percent. This was the first time in twenty years that voter turnout in a New Jersey congressional election had been higher than that of the preceding gubernatorial election. The Department of State credits mail registration for the increase.[5] It should be noted, however, that the number of registered voters was smaller in 1974 than in 1973. Voter turnout for the past five election years in New Jersey is presented in Table 11.

Reactions of Officials to the Mail-Registration System. In contrast to Maryland election officials, who were very heavily in favor of the mail-registration system in effect in that state, New Jersey election officials were of mixed opinions on their procedures. Some said they preferred the mail-registration system because it reduced the volume of last minute registration, but others reported that the registration

---

[5] New Jersey Department of State, *Annual Report for Calendar Year 1974*, p. 26.

Table 11

VOTER TURNOUT IN NEW JERSEY BY COUNTY, 1970–1974

(in thousands)

	1974	1973	1972	1971	1970	Percent Increase or Decrease, 1970–1974
Atlantic	67	60	78	69	60	+ 11.6
Bergen	312	314	444	306	334	− 6.5
Burlington	89	80	111	75	76	+ 17.0
Camden	143	129	193	133	131	+ 9.1
Cape May	29	27	30	24	23	+ 26.1
Cumberland	37	34	42	32	34	+ 8.8
Essex	209	240	348	215	235	− 11.0
Gloucester	59	53	74	52	56	+ 5.3
Hudson	146	166	233	185	181	− 19.3
Hunterdon	23	22	29	19	21	+ 9.5
Mercer	96	97	136	84	97	− 1.0
Middlesex	170	176	246	167	172	− 1.2
Monmouth	150	141	193	129	138	+ 8.6
Morris	119	115	160	102	114	+ 4.3
Ocean	98	88	109	72	69	+ 42.0
Passaic	118	123	172	108	125	− 5.6
Salem	21	19	24	19	20	+ 5.0
Somerset	65	63	86	54	61	+ 6.5
Sussex	27	25	33	22	23	+ 17.3
Union	172	171	247	164	188	− 8.5
Warren	23	22	30	20	22	+ 4.5
Total for state	2,183	2,175	3,030	2,062	2,209	− 1.1

Source: Turnout data from Elections Section, New Jersey Department of State.

forms delivered by parties and groups near the deadline or even afterward made their work more difficult. Several officials believed that the system required additional work in verifying signatures of witnesses and in handling both the mail-registration form and the permanent records.

One official complained that the mail-registration form had to be cut and pasted to a permanent record so that the signature comparison could be made at the polling place. Several believed that the law had been implemented too quickly and that procedures were not clear. Several expressed fear of possible fraud, while others pointed out that the signature check helped guard against fraudulent registrations.

Other local officials, county clerks, and municipal clerks were also divided in their evaluations of the effectiveness and the integrity of the mail-registration system. Depending upon the experience of their own jurisdictions, they believed that mail registration did or did not increase voter registration and voter turnout.

Merrill Montgomery, a clerk in Little Falls township who is also chairman of the International Institute of Municipal Clerks subcommittee on postcard voter registration, reported that the New Jersey mail-registration system is "something that the clerks can live with."[6] Although a straw vote taken at the annual conference of the New Jersey League of Municipalities indicated that a substantial majority of the clerks favored abolition of mail registration, Montgomery reported that most believed that the complications had not been quite as severe as had been anticipated. She cited instances of three fourteen-year-olds registering to vote by mail in Union County in order to obtain proof of age on the basis of which they might procure alcoholic beverage identification cards. She also noted that voters who had given less than complete and accurate addresses had found themselves at the wrong polling place on election day, even in as small a community as Little Falls.

In general, New Jersey election officials who were skeptical of mail registration when it was introduced are less so now. Several would like to see mail registration replace entirely the registration days and hours now required by law. There is, however, great concern about the possibility of federal mail registration. Local officials are apprehensive about federal oversight of local registration, mass duplication of registrations, and general administrative problems.

---

[6] Telephone interview with Merrill Montgomery, 11 February 1975.

4
COMPARATIVE ANALYSIS

How well did the mail-registration systems in Maryland and New Jersey work during 1974? An attempt is made here to evaluate the success of mail registration in registering voters, to find out whether voters who register by mail are more likely than others to vote, and to discover whether mail registration has an impact on political party registration. The cost of the system and its administration—including problems such as duplicate registrations, illegible applications, and locating voters who do not declare street addresses—are also analyzed. Most importantly, the safeguards against vote fraud are carefully assessed, and the misuses of voter-registration identification cards that have come to light are described.

Mail Registration and Participation in the Electoral Process

Impact of Mail Registration on Numbers Registered. If it is assumed that registration constitutes "an administrative obstacle to voting," [1] that people fail to register because registration points are few and far between, hours inconvenient, and forms and procedures complicated, then the introduction of a simple voter-registration-by-mail system should be accompanied by a sharp increase in the number of registered voters. This increase did not occur in Maryland or New Jersey. Instead, the number of voters registered in New Jersey as of November 1974 was 39,000 fewer than the number on the registry for the 1973 gubernatorial election, and the number of registered voters in Maryland in November 1974 was 77,000 fewer than the number on

---

[1] Administrative obstacles to voter registration are identified in "Administrative Obstacles to Voting," a report of the Election Systems Project, League of Women Voters Educational Fund, Washington, D. C., 1972.

the registry for 1972, the most recent election year. Interest in the candidates and in the offices being contested clearly has a stronger effect on voter registration than the actual procedure for registration. (Total voter registration in Maryland and New Jersey counties for all election years since 1970 is shown in Tables 12 and 13.)

An analysis of "comparable year" statistics also makes it appear unlikely that mail registration significantly increased voter registration in New Jersey during 1974. The most recent nonpresidential federal election year prior to 1974 was 1970. New Jersey's total voter registration for the election of 1970 was 97 percent of what it had been for 1969, a gubernatorial election year, and its total voter registration for the election of 1974 was 98 percent of the 1973 gubernatorial registration. The figures are strikingly similar, the slight difference as easily accounted for by population growth as by mail registration. The change in the minimum voting age does not distort this comparison since eighteen-year-olds were ineligible to vote in both 1969 and 1970, and eligible in both 1973 and 1974.

New Jersey reported registering 135,957 new voters during 1974, 3.9 percent of its total registration. This figure, however, was insufficient to offset the deletions from the rolls caused by death, removal from the county of residence, and disfranchisement.

Maryland did not have an election in 1973 and figures for the presidential election of 1972 are not truly comparable. Nevertheless, the total registration in Maryland *declined* by more than 77,000 voters between 1972 and 1974 despite the introduction of mail registration. In fact, over two-thirds of the decline (about 55,000) occurred in two mail-registration jurisdictions, Baltimore City and Prince George's County. The decline was in part the result of the five-year purge which removed the names of persons who had not voted in the 1968 presidential election or since.

Even in the Maryland counties which had the best records for voter registration between 1972 and 1974, mail registration appears to have had relatively little impact on numbers registered. Despite large population increases in Montgomery County during the last four years, the number of new registrants over twenty-one years of age was 23,138 in 1974, compared with 21,788 in 1970. Persons under twenty-one were still ineligible to vote in 1970, and the registration of persons under twenty-one accounts for almost all of the increase in registration between 1970 and 1974.

Harford and Howard counties indicated increases in voter registration between 1972 and 1974. Both of these smaller counties have experienced very high *rates of growth* during the past four years.

Table 12
VOTER REGISTRATION IN NEW JERSEY BY COUNTY, 1970–1974
(in thousands)

	1974	1973	1972	1971	1970	Percent Increase or Decrease 1973–1974
Atlantic	94	91	93	87	84	+ 3.3
Bergen	481	495	519	478	451	− 2.8
Burlington	134	132	138	119	110	+ 1.5
Camden	228	242	249	221	214	− 5.8
Cape May	41	40	39	34	31	+ 2.5
Cumberland	55	55	56	53	50	
Essex	390	397	420	392	389	− 1.8
Gloucester	87	84	87	80	76	+ 3.6
Hudson	270	279	290	281	265	− 3.2
Hunterdon	34	35	36	32	30	− 2.9
Mercer	160	156	164	146	139	+ 2.6
Middlesex	282	296	298	272	250	− 4.7
Monmouth	225	226	230	204	191	− 0.4
Morris	189	189	196	172	160	
Ocean	141	130	125	102	94	+ 8.5
Passaic	198	203	215	196	189	− 2.4
Salem	30	30	32	30	29	
Somerset	100	99	103	89	84	+ 1.0
Sussex	40	40	41	35	33	
Union	277	280	295	269	258	− 1.1
Warren	34	34	35	32	31	
State total	3,502	3,541	3,672	3,334	3,167	− 1.1

Source: New Jersey Department of State.

59

Table 13
TOTAL VOTER REGISTRATION AND REGISTERED VOTERS VOTING IN MARYLAND BY COUNTY, 1970–1974

	1974		1972		1970	
	Registration (in thousands)	Percent voted	Registration (in thousands)	Percent voted	Registration (in thousands)	Percent voted
Mail-registration counties						
Baltimore City	389	41.6	424	62.3	435	46.7
Harford County	51	57.9	47	72.8	87	68.8
Howard County	42	60.5	38	79.1	24	69.1
Montgomery County	291	56.9	294	80.2	222	71.1
Prince George's County	215	54.5	238	83.3	212	61.7
Total, mail-registration counties	988	51.0	1,041	73.2	930	57.4
Total, all other counties	749	59.3	774	76.2	664	66.0
Total, Maryland	1,737	54.6	1,815	74.5	1,594	61.0

Source: Maryland State Administrative Board of Election Laws.

Because each of them has large newly developed communities, purges for nonvoting and for moving from the county removed very few names from the lists in 1972. In Prince George's County, however, despite large population growth, *new* registration declined between 1970 and 1974.

Nevertheless, there is some evidence that mail registration contributed to slight increases in voter registration in some places. Marie Garber, election administrator for Montgomery County since 1967, believes that mail registration was responsible for about a 10 percent increase in *new* registrations during 1974. Without mail registration, she estimates, some 2,000 to 3,000 fewer persons would have registered. If this is true, the introduction of mail registration accounts for a net increase of about 1 percent in the total Montgomery County registration.

Some New Jersey counties increased voter-registration totals between 1973 and 1974, and some county officials gave mail registration credit for part of that increase. Yet, there were also twelve New Jersey counties which experienced absolute decreases in registered voters during the same period. Interviews with officials in all New Jersey counties suggest that vigorous recruitment by candidates and political party groups who took advantage of the new registration procedure accounted for most of the increases. Mail registration without partisan registration drives failed to produce increases.[2]

If the numbers of voters who registered during *similar periods* in 1970 and 1974 are compared, some dramatic increases appear to exist. Early in 1974 there were reports that mail registration had greatly increased voter registration in Maryland, but these figures covered only the first few months of the year, long before an election. During the base period of 1970, very few persons had registered.

New Jersey reported that mail registration had "more than doubled new registrations" in 1974, as compared to 1970.[3] The actual extent of the increase is not easily determined, however. As noted in Chapter 3, some transactions that were counted as "mail registrations" were not, in fact, new registrations. After all the new registrations had been recorded, the total number of registered voters turned out to be 39,000 fewer than in 1973.

---

[2] Kevin P. Phillips and Paul H. Blackman, *Electoral Reform and Voter Participation* (Washington, D. C.: American Enterprise Institute, 1975), pp. 61–65, describe efforts in other states.

[3] Official news release from New Jersey Department of State, undated but distributed November 1974.

Variations in voter registration and in voter turnout between presidential and nonpresidential election years clearly demonstrate that it is voter interest in candidates, offices, and issues, rather than the method of registration, that determines whether or not people register. The implementation of mail registration in Maryland and New Jersey was not the cause of reduced voter registration between 1974 and the preceding general election year, and it will not be the cause of increased voter registration between 1974 and the presidential election of 1976. A successful mail-registration program which supplements existing registration practices may increase the total number of eligible voters in a jurisdiction one or two percentage points. But the experience of Maryland and New Jersey so far suggests that mail registration is unlikely to produce dramatic increases in voter-registration totals.

Mail Registration and Voter Turnout. The relationship between mail registration and voter turnout is more difficult to establish. Maryland kept track of whether mail registrants actually voted, so there is no doubt about what happened in most of the five counties. However, New Jersey did not, so conclusions must be inferred from voter turnout data. This is difficult in New Jersey where the number of new registrants in most counties was a very small proportion of the electorate.

In Maryland, voters who registered by mail came to the polls in approximately the same numbers as those who registered in person. In Howard County the turnout of mail registrants was higher than that of voters who registered in person (see Table 14). In Prince George's County it was about five percentage points less. Montgomery County did not maintain statistics on mail registrants, only because all registrants used the mail-registration form, but the turnout of voters newly registered in 1974 was approximately the same as that of voters who had registered prior to 1974.

Although there are no figures from New Jersey, reports of local officials and inferences from the data suggest that the result was similar. The number of registered voters declined between 1973 and 1974 by 39,000, but the number of voters voting increased by about 8,000. The percentage of voters voting in the state as a whole increased from 61.4 percent to 62.3 percent. Although increases in voter turnout generally occurred in counties with large registration increases in 1974, this was not always the case (see Table 15). Even though voter registration had increased some 335,000 between 1970 and 1974, there were 25,000 fewer voters at the polls in 1974 than in

Table 14

TURNOUT OF MAIL REGISTRANTS IN HOWARD COUNTY, BY PRECINCT, 1974

District and Precinct		Number Registered	Number Voting	Percent
District 1:	1	182	108	59.34
	2	43	25	58.14
	3	118	57	48.31
Total		343	190	55.39
District 2:	1	162	108	66.67
	2	89	52	58.43
	3	62	42	67.74
	4	177	110	62.15
	5	94	66	70.21
	6	67	53	79.10
	7	70	56	80.00
	8	28	20	71.43
	9	309	181	58.58
	10	47	30	63.83
	11	90	56	62.22
Total		1,195	774	64.77
District 3		200	143	71.50
District 4:	1	80	53	66.25
	2	68	48	70.59
Total		148	101	68.24
District 5:	1	104	74	71.15
	2	261	167	63.98
	3	303	238	78.55
	4	371	257	69.21
	5	75	49	65.33
	6	56	35	62.50
	7	458	294	64.19
	8	183	125	68.31
Total		1,811	1,239	68.42
District 6:	1	24	19	79.17
	2	280	161	57.50
	3	54	40	74.07
	4	114	74	64.91
	5	817	548	67.07
	6	163	130	79.75
	7	23	12	52.17
	8	299	214	71.57
	9	520	375	72.42
	10	1,002	668	66.67
Total		3,296	2,241	67.99
Total for county		6,993	4,688	67.04

Source: Howard County Board of Supervisors of Elections.

Table 15
NEW REGISTRANTS AND VOTER TURNOUT IN NEW JERSEY, BY COUNTY, 1973–1974

| | Percent of Registered Voters Voting | | Difference in Percent of Registered Voters Voting, 1973–1974 | New Registrants as a Percent of Total Registration in County |
	1973	1974		
Atlantic	66.2	71.9	+5.7	5.1
Bergen	63.8	64.8	+1.0	2.4
Burlington	61.0	66.2	+5.2	5.6
Camden	53.5	62.7	+9.2	7.6
Cape May	69.1	71.5	+1.6	4.2
Cumberland	62.9	68.5	+5.6	3.8
Essex	60.4	53.6	−6.8	1.6
Gloucester	63.9	67.8	+3.9	5.8
Hudson	59.8	54.0	−5.4	3.3
Hunterdon	62.6	67.5	+4.9	3.5
Mercer	62.3	60.3	−2.0	3.9
Middlesex	58.8	60.2	+1.4	4.6
Monmouth	62.8	66.7	+3.9	4.2
Morris	60.7	63.0	+2.3	4.4
Ocean	68.3	69.5	+1.2	6.9
Passaic	60.7	59.9	−0.8	1.7
Salem	64.8	69.2	+4.4	5.3
Somerset	63.7	65.4	+1.7	4.7
Sussex	63.6	67.6	+4.0	5.9
Union	61.3	62.0	+0.7	2.7
Warren	63.3	66.7	+3.4	3.1
NEW JERSEY	61.4	62.3	+0.9	3.9

Source: New Jersey Department of State provided percent of registered voters voting; other calculations made from figures supplied by the Department of State.

1970. All New Jersey counties, with the exception of three small counties and Camden County, had a decrease between 1970 and 1974 in the proportion of registered voters actually voting (see Table 16). The Camden increase is notable because Camden, a large county, also had the largest percentage of new registrants in 1974.

One conclusion seems obvious. Persons who register to vote by mail during an election year are no more likely to vote than those who

Table 16

TURNOUT OF REGISTERED VOTERS IN NEW JERSEY, BY COUNTY, 1970 AND 1974

	1974	1970
Atlantic	71.9	71.8
Bergen	64.8	74.0
Burlington	66.2	69.3
Camden	62.7	61.5
Cape May	71.5	76.0
Cumberland	68.5	67.5
Essex	53.6	64.9
Gloucester	67.8	74.2
Hudson	54.0	68.5
Hunterdon	67.5	70.8
Mercer	60.3	69.7
Middlesex	60.2	68.7
Monmouth	66.7	72.3
Morris	63.0	71.1
Ocean	69.5	73.7
Passaic	59.9	66.5
Salem	69.2	68.2
Somerset	65.4	72.5
Sussex	67.6	70.6
Union	62.0	73.0
Warren	66.7	71.5
NEW JERSEY	62.3	69.7

Source: New Jersey Department of State.

are already on the books. This contradicts a widely held belief that *new registrants* are more likely to vote. Whether it would hold true in a state without mail registration is not known.

Mail Registration and Party Affiliation. There is little evidence thus far to support the contention that mail registration favors one party. New Jersey does not provide for voter registration by party, and the results of a single election are an insufficient basis from which to draw a conclusion. In Maryland, where party registration is required, it is possible that voter registration by mail may be related to an increase in the proportion of registrants who fail to designate any party preference and who thus deny themselves the opportunity of participating in primary elections. Not all the mail-registration counties maintained statistics by political party, but the overall pattern of voter registration by party in the state indicates that the direction of party registration in the counties with mail registration and those without has been similar (see Table 17).

The total voter registration by party within the five jurisdictions using voter registration by mail also reveals little basis for concluding that mail registration assisted either party to any great extent. Democratic registration in Baltimore City did increase from 83.2 percent in 1972 to 84.4 percent in 1974, but this is accounted for in part

Table 17

VOTER REGISTRATION BY POLITICAL PARTY IN MARYLAND
COUNTIES WITH MAIL REGISTRATION, 1970–1974

| | | Percentage Distribution | | |
		1974	1972	1970
Baltimore City	Democrat	84.4	83.2	82.1
	Republican	12.8	14.6	16.1
	Decline	2.6	2.0	1.7
Harford	Democrat	68.2	67.0	68.8
	Republican	27.8	29.4	28.4
	Decline	3.7	3.3	2.6
Howard	Democrat	63.7	62.9	63.3
	Republican	29.6	31.7	33.8
	Decline	6.5	5.2	2.8
Montgomery	Democrat	59.4	58.9	59.3
	Republican	31.8	33.4	34.4
	Decline	8.6	7.7	6.2
Prince George's	Democrat	66.7	66.1	66.3
	Republican	26.6	27.9	28.3
	Decline	6.5	5.9	5.2
Maryland counties with mail regis- tration	Democrat	71.6	71.0	72.7
	Republican	23.0	24.2	23.6
	Decline	5.4	4.7	3.7
Maryland counties without mail registration	Democrat	67.6	67.2	67.5
	Republican	29.2	29.8	30.5
	Decline	3.2	2.9	2.9
Maryland	Democrat	69.8	69.4	70.5
	Republican	25.6	26.6	26.4
	Decline	4.5	3.9	2.9

Source: Based upon registration figures provided by the State Administrative Board of Election Laws.

by population changes. The black population of this heavily Democratic city increased during this period, and the white population declined. In the other four jurisdictions, the percentage of the registered voters who were Democrats was almost identical with what it had been in 1970. The percentage of Republicans declined in all five jurisdictions between 1972 and 1974 at about the same rate as between 1970 and 1972.

Some counties maintained statistics on political party affiliation of persons who registered by mail and in person during 1974 (see Table 18). There were more "declines" and considerably fewer Republicans among voters who registered by mail in Prince George's and Harford counties. In all Maryland counties, a voter who registers in person who declines to state a party preference is advised that unless he does so he will not be permitted to vote in primary elections. This information frequently prompts the registrant to affiliate with one of the major political parties. Local officials suggest that the

Table 18

NEW VOTER REGISTRATION BY PARTY, POSTCARD AND IN PERSON, FOR HARFORD, MONTGOMERY, AND PRINCE GEORGE'S COUNTIES, 1974

	Postcard		In Person		Total during 1974	
Harford	(62%)		(38%)		(100%)	
Democrat	2,335	75%	1,266	66%	3,601	71%
Republican	596	19%	576	30%	1,172	23%
Decline	198	6%	83	4%	281	6%
Total	3,129		1,915		5,054	
Montgomery	(60%)		(40%)		(100%)	
Democrat	10,367	59%	6,942	60%	17,309	60%
Republican	3,753	21%	2,474	24%	6,498	22%
Decline	3,403	19%	1,896	16%	5,272	18%
Total	17,523		11,558		29,079	
Prince George's	(56%)		(44%)		(100%)	
Democrat	9,453	67%	7,539	67%	16,992	67%
Republican	2,052	15%	2,507	22%	4,559	18%
Decline	2,612	18%	1,063	10%	3,675	15%
Total	14,121		11,171		25,292	

Source: Boards of supervisors of elections of Harford, Montgomery, and Prince George's counties.

failure to realize this fact and a reluctance to identify with the Republican party at this time may produce the effect shown in Table 18.

Cost of Registration by Mail

The cost of voter registration includes all expenses related to obtaining information from prospective voters, processing it, and maintaining current and accurate lists of registered voters. Cost estimates are most difficult to obtain because systems of records and accounts vary from one jurisdiction to another. Some cost estimates fail to include mailing, data processing, printing, supplementary help provided by the general county government, or other factors which must be considered. It is possible, however, to single out specific factors related to voter registration and to compare their costs under the mail-registration and the traditional systems.

Both Maryland and New Jersey have more expensive methods of registering voters than most other states.[4] Maryland has long required that two registrars, a Democrat and a Republican, complete a registration card for every registrant. This requirement is still in effect in non-mail-registration situations. Further, both Maryland and New Jersey send registrars to field locations, an extremely expensive and relatively unproductive procedure. The cost of field registration was over $10 per registered voter in some New Jersey municipalities, and much higher in others. In Ewing (Mercer County) twelve voters were registered in forty-seven hours at a cost of $20.08 per registrant; in Pennington (Mercer County) six registrants in fifty hours at a cost of $36.66 per registrant; and in North Haledon (Passaic County) seven voters at a cost per registrant of $46.40.[5] Anything which replaces this procedure is very likely to save money.

Mail registration has proved to be no more expensive than previous methods in any county, and much less expensive in most counties in Maryland and New Jersey. The cost of registration by mail is estimated to be about $2.00 per registered voter in Howard County, Maryland. This was the highest estimate received for any county, and equalled the estimated cost per registrant of non-mail registration in Howard County. The lowest estimate was about fifty cents per registered voter in Baltimore City and in several New Jersey counties. New Jersey state law provides a rebate to counties of fifty cents per registered voter, but Assistant Secretary of State F. Joseph

---

[4] Richard G. Smolka, *The Costs of Administering American Elections* (New York: National Municipal League, 1973), Chapter 4.

[5] Figures for municipalities provided by the Department of State of New Jersey.

Carragher believes that, when all factors are considered, expenses to the county are probably closer to $1.00. A recent study reached similar conclusions.[6]

Mail registration requires that voter-registration cards have to be printed and then have to be distributed either by mail or by unpaid deputies. If the local jurisdiction provides postage-paid forms, there is an additional cost of about eleven cents per registered voter. This covers ten cents postage and a certain amount of duplication. The voter-notification form adds an additional eight cents to ten cents to the cost. In New Jersey administrative time is required to verify the signatures of witnesses, to investigate the addresses of persons whose voter-notification cards are returned, and to locate the election district and polling place of each registered voter. Maryland has all of these expenses except for verification of the witness and personal investigation.

Some Maryland counties have further reduced their costs by using the original mail voter-registration card in the file. Others transcribe the information onto another type of card for use at the polls, or transfer it to automatic data processing equipment. When this is done, administrative costs are about the same as with non-mail registration systems. Counties which have initiated around-the-clock telephone answering services report great savings over the field-location system.

To the extent that mail registration replaces rather than supplements the traditional systems in Maryland and New Jersey, costs are reduced. Expensive and unproductive personal registration locations may be abandoned without eliminating the service they provided simply by making it possible for a voter to obtain a form without the presence of two or more paid deputy registrars. Distribution of the forms by party groups who serve as unpaid deputies also reduces costs. Even if the number of registrations increases dramatically, it should cost less to register voters by mail than by the current system.

Whether or not mail registration will decrease expenses in other states depends upon what the state is currently spending to register voters. In Minnesota, which previously had no voter registration in some areas, the cost to register voters has obviously increased. In states such as New York and Ohio, which have voter-registration systems similar to that of New Jersey, mail registration would probably reduce expenses. Mail registration is neither the least expensive nor the most expensive method of obtaining the names of eligible voters.

---

[6] Smolka, *The Costs of Administering American Elections.*

The cost of mail-registration systems is affected, of course, by whether postage-paid application forms are used. The four Maryland counties required prospective registrants to affix postage stamps to their mail-registration forms, whereas Baltimore City and the New Jersey counties provided postage-paid forms. The Maryland counties justified their requirement that the registrant pay the postage on two grounds—cost and the prevention of the mischievous use of the forms. Some officials also maintain that the voter should demonstrate an interest in registering to vote at least to the extent of paying the price of a postage stamp or returning the registration form in person. Advocates of the post-paid form argue that it increases the probability that people will register without greatly adding to the cost of registration. They say that substantial numbers of people simply mislay their forms or forget to mail them because they do not have postage stamps readily available. (Approximately one-third of the registration forms sent out in response to letter or telephone requests are not returned.) [7] Both Baltimore City and New Jersey's counties report that the incidence of duplicate registrations, frivolous information, blank forms, and obscene scribblings was minimal. No jurisdiction reported more than 350 such instances. Critics of postage-paid forms, of course, are concerned not only about the postage but also about the cost of processing mischievous forms which appear correct and of attempting to track down and identify fictitious persons. Thus far, however, there is no evidence that such mischief has occurred under either system.

Administrative Factors Related to Mail Registration

In testimony before Congress, state and local officials cited several possible administrative difficulties of voter registration by mail.[8] These included illegible applications, duplicate registrations, problems in attempting to locate the correct addresses of voters who used RFD or post office boxes, and a heavy volume of registrations just prior to the close of the books. These problems would beset federal and state mail-registration systems equally.

Local officials also cited administrative problems that would only arise if mail registration were implemented by the federal government.

---

[7] See Chapter 2. Even more surprising was the fact that 639 of the 1,014 students at the University of Maryland who requested voter-registration forms failed to return them.

[8] U.S. Congress, House of Representatives, Subcommittee on Elections of the Committee on House Administration, *Hearings on the Voter Registration Act and Related Legislation*, 93rd Congress, 1st session, June and July 1973.

These included the maintenance of dual registration lists, one for federal voters and the other for voters eligible to participate in all elections. Congress can make laws pertaining only to federal elections, and states that did not extend the federal system to local and state elections would be obliged to maintain two sets of records. The relationship between a federal voter-registration agency and the local registrars also seemed problematical.

Election officials in New Jersey and Maryland reported little difficulty with voter handwriting. Although many had expressed fear that long hours would be required to decipher handwriting, experience demonstrated that registrants, assisted by trained volunteers in Maryland or unpaid deputies in New Jersey, were careful to write clearly. This was so striking that several officials commented that the forms were easier to process than those filled out by paid deputies. In Maryland, registrars had been required to fill out each and every form, and after an hour or two their handwriting had deteriorated badly. The forms used by Maryland and New Jersey are simple and voters experienced little difficulty in providing complete information in the spaces provided.

Maryland officials reported that less than 1 percent of all mail registrations duplicated existing registrations. For New Jersey there are no comparable figures because some officials honored all registrations and reported no duplicates. Camden County and Monmouth County each reported about 300 duplications, about 2 percent of all mail registrations in Camden County and about 5 percent in Monmouth County. Other counties recorded fewer duplications or none at all.

Several officials in Maryland and New Jersey had expressed fear that voter registration by mail would be complicated by the use of nonresidence addresses and post office boxes or the complete absence of street addresses. In such cases, it was feared, much additional work would be required to determine precisely where the registrant was eligible to vote. This problem appears to have been resolved with minimum difficulty in both states.

If there is any doubt about the exact location of the residence of the voter, more information is requested. Maryland has provided a form for this purpose, and Maryland and New Jersey both make inquiries by telephone. New Jersey, on occasion, sends an investigator to locate the residence address.

Mail registration can significantly reduce the proportion of voters who register in the peak periods prior to elections. Table 19 indicates the distribution of voter registrations for Montgomery County, Mary-

Table 19

NEW VOTER REGISTRATION IN MONTGOMERY COUNTY, MARYLAND, BY MONTH, 1970 AND 1974

	1970			1974	
	Number of voters registered	Percentage of total registrations		Number of voters registered	Percentage of total registrations
January	369	2	January	1,495	5
February	445	2	February	1,412	5
March	721	3	March	1,641	6
April	858	4	April	1,350	5
May	1,353	6	May	3,520 [a]	12
June	1,659	7	June	1,401	5
July	2,361	11	July	2,694	9
August (to 8/17)	6,783	31	August (to 8/12)	6,592	23
September 26– October 5	6,550	30	September 23– October 7	7,815	27
November	236	1	November	773	2
December	686 [b]	3	December	386	1
	22,021 (of which 283 were under 21)			29,079 (of which 5,941 were under 21)	

[a] Includes 2,348 school registrations.
[b] Persons under twenty-one were permitted to register in December 1970 for the first time.
Source: Montgomery County Board of Supervisors of Elections.

land, by month for the years 1970 and 1974. During 1974, 47 percent of the annual registration had been effected by the end of July, whereas in 1970 only 35 percent of the registration had been accomplished by that date. Election officials in Maryland were unanimous in reporting that there were no long lines at the close of voter registration prior to either the primary or the general election. In New Jersey, however, some officials were confronted with large numbers of voter-registration forms delivered by political parties and groups near and after the close of registration prior to the general election.

Election officials also reported that mail registration eliminated charges of political favoritism, sectional favoritism, and racial discrimination in the choice of sites for personal registration. In past years, political parties, groups, and candidates had complained that the locations and hours of the registration facilities had favored some party or group, but no complaints of this type were voiced in any mail-registration county in Maryland or New Jersey.

The Potential for Vote Fraud

In neither Maryland nor New Jersey has there been any systematic attempt to determine the incidence of fraudulent registration and in neither state has vote fraud resulting from fraudulent registration been reported.

New Jersey's Safeguard. In New Jersey, the safeguards against vote fraud resulting from mail registration include the requirement of a witness on the mail-registration form, the nonforwardable voter-notification form, the signature at the polling place, widespread dissemination of the election district voter-registration lists to the parties (who may challenge persons believed to be improperly registered), and the small scale of the election districts (the average number of registered voters per election district is 641).

In practice the signature of a witness who is a registered voter in New Jersey is not always verified. In fact, the court ruling that ended the Monmouth County controversy described in Chapter 3 established that the witness's signature is not essential. The nonforwardable voter-notification form, on the other hand, does provide a check on most registrants. The postal service does return most notifications which are undeliverable as addressed. When a voter-notification card is returned, the action taken varies by county, as described in Chapters 2 and 3.

New Jersey requires a signature at the polls each time a person votes, which provides a continuing check, although election officials in several states including Maryland have serious doubts about the ability of unskilled polling-place officials to determine whether one signature is sufficiently different from the signature in the books to disqualify a person from voting. A signature check is also made by the county clerk in cooperation with the commissioner of registration if an absentee ballot is requested.

Mail registration combined with absentee voting provides an opportunity for vote fraud without personal challenge or personal recognition by any election official. Although a signature check is made, as long as the signature of the applicant for a ballot matches that of the registrant, the ballot is sent and will be counted. Once he has received his ballot, a fraudulent voter need never return to the address to which it had been sent. In fact, if it is possible for a person to receive mail inconspicuously at an address, he need not even reside there to perpetrate vote fraud. It would actually be possible to obtain absentee ballots from several counties in a single state and to vote in each without ever setting foot within the state. Theoretically, the same thing could be done in states without mail registration but which permit absentee registration, but it would be more difficult to accomplish since far fewer people register absentee. The potential for fraud of this type is increased in direct proportion to the volume of mail registrations. Against this practice the signature check offers little protection.

In neither Maryland nor New Jersey did any election official know the number of absentee ballots sent to persons who registered by mail. In some jurisdictions it could be determined by comparing the absentee-voters list with the registered-voters list, but in others once the voter had been placed on the registration list it was impossible to determine whether he had registered in person or by mail. Local officials stated that they were far too busy during the period just prior to the election to pay much attention to this relationship. It is uncertain whether mail registration is associated with absentee voting in numbers sufficient to warrant investigation.

Dissemination of the voter-registration lists to the parties and candidates in New Jersey does offer potential for restricting vote fraud. This potential is realized only if there is a vigorous effort on the part of the political parties to ensure that only registered voters are permitted to vote. In the 1972 Democratic primary election for Congress in which John Rooney (D-New York) and Allard Lowenstein were the candidates, both sides actively scrutinized the lists of registered voters and challenged many. Without a vigorous party or candidate organization, however, posting the lists of registered voters in each election district does little to discourage fraud.

A small election district or precinct is a definite deterrent to vote fraud. The fewer the registered voters per election district, the greater the likelihood that the identity of the voters will be known to the polling place officials. It is also more likely that an unusually high number of votes cast in a small precinct will cause suspicion and investigation. In some states, to increase the probability of voter identification, polling place officials must reside in the election district in which they serve, but this is not the situation in New Jersey. It is difficult to recruit a sufficient number of capable officials in every election district, and the smaller the election district, the less likely that all officials will be residents of the district in which they serve.

Through a simple mechanism, New Jersey maintains a list of registered voters which is more current and more accurate than that of most states. Nonforwardable sample ballots are sent to all registered voters in June and November. Undeliverable sample ballots are returned to the county clerk or appropriate official who removes the voters from the rolls under the provisions of the law. Voters who move are unlikely to remain on the books in New Jersey for more than one year. The New Jersey system, however, does not conscientiously ensure that new voters are removed from the lists in their former election districts, especially if they have come from out of state.

Maryland's Safeguard. The Maryland safeguards against vote fraud through mail registration begin with control over the distribution of the voter-registration form. All mail-registration jurisdictions in Maryland were able to identify and monitor the performance of groups which distributed mail-registration forms during 1974. There was no reason to suspect that fraudulent registrations had been generated by any group. In fact, far more voter registrations resulted from individual requests by telephone or in person than from party or group activity.

Maryland, too, uses the nonforwardable voter-notification form as a check on the identification and the residence of the registrant. (See pages 78–80 for a discussion of a test of this process.) Although the law and rules provide that a voter is not registered unless and until the voter-notification form has been received, some counties did place the name of the voter in the precinct file as soon as his registration form had been received by the office, and before the voter-notification form had been sent.

Maryland's precincts, with the exception of those in Baltimore City, usually contain several hundred more voters than do election districts in New Jersey (see Table 9). As a result, there is less likelihood of precinct officials recognizing voters at the polls in Maryland. Precinct lists are made available in Maryland, but they must be purchased, and are not publicly posted as in New Jersey. Still, the active political parties and candidates are able to scrutinize them for possible inaccuracies.

Maryland does not mail sample ballots or other information to all registered voters on a regular basis. The purge in Baltimore City described on page 27 indicates how out-of-date a voter-registration list may become. Prince George's has had more frequent general mailings than other jurisdictions during the past five years and as a result has purged far more voters. In most counties in Maryland, voters who move are quite likely to remain on the books for at least five years before being purged for nonvoting, unless they attempt to register at new addresses within the state.

Maryland does have a precinct signature check in some counties, but the general trend is toward the use of electronically produced precinct lists. Personal identification rather than signature comparison is required when electronically produced books are sent to precincts. This has the disadvantage that it does not force imposters to forge signatures, and signatures forged at the polling places have often been used as evidence in the successful prosecution of vote fraud.

The potential for vote fraud in Maryland or New Jersey or any other state is directly dependent upon the volume and timing of mail registrations. Maryland closes its books thirty days prior to an election. Registration forms not received by the close of the books, or forms which are received but are incomplete, are not included in the precinct books for the immediate election. New Jersey, by accepting forms as much as one week after the close of the books, makes the task of the election official more difficult. What's more, when registration forms may be deposited in substantial numbers by interested parties or candidates, the motivation as well as the opportunity for fraud is increased.

Assistant Secretary of State F. Joseph Carragher of New Jersey argues that the mail-registration system actually reduces the chances of fraud because it requires a witness and immediate mail notification. Some Maryland officials, too, believe that fraud may be easier to perpetrate under the personal voter-registration system since there is no mail notification for voters who register in person. It is true that a single person can fraudulently register once, more easily under the personal registration systems, but it would be extremely difficult for him to register several times without being recognized. The mail-voter-registration system would allow one person to register fraudulently any number of times from the privacy of his own room, even out of state. A very small conspiracy could be very productive. The weaknesses of the administrative process in New Jersey make it difficult to discover any fraud perpetrated immediately prior to the close of the books.

The mail-voter-registration system demands greater attention to detail than the personal-registration system if it is to protect the election process from fraud. If the system becomes lax and audits are not made, wholesale vote fraud is a distinct possibility.

Most election officials expressed no fear of fraud in federal elections, when the number of votes cast is too high to make it worth the risk. They were more concerned about the danger of false registration and voting in local contests, particularly in wards where a few hundred votes can mean the difference between winning and losing. Most of the vote scandals reported by Joseph Harris years ago involved local, not federal, elections, and it is in local elections that the fruits of crime may seem to make the risk of conviction of a misdemeanor worth the risk.[9]

The accurate delivery of the voter-notification form and the return of the form if the registrant does not reside at the address indicated are essential to the fraud protection systems prescribed in Maryland and New Jersey law. Inaccurate delivery can produce two types of errors. If the voter-notification form is not delivered to a registrant who, in fact, lives at the address indicated, that registrant may be removed from the registry erroneously and denied the opportunity to vote. At the very least, he will not be informed officially of his election district or precinct and the location of his polling place. Alternatively, if the voter-notification form is not returned to the election office, the name of the registrant remains on the books even though there may be no such person at the address shown on the registration form.

One problem that does not arise is the U.S. Postal Service's improperly returning notification forms of persons who actually live at the addresses on the forms. Very few voter-notification forms were returned in New Jersey: only three counties reported over 100 returns and several reported considerably fewer. Out of 82,932 notifications issued in Maryland, only 242 were returned by the postal service as undeliverable. Of these, 203 were in Baltimore City. In most cases there had been an error in transcribing the address of the registrant or in transmitting the information to data processing. Some forms were returned because the applicants had failed to provide complete addresses. Omission of the apartment number appeared to be the most common mistake. These errors were sometimes corrected by telephone inquiry or at the polls on election day. In Prince George's County, where 24 voter-notification forms were returned out of

9 Joseph P. Harris, *Registration of Voters in the United States*, Chapter 1.

14,485, several forms were not delivered owing to changes in street numbers by the local government. In three other Maryland jurisdictions very few notification forms were returned. Only 2 forms were returned in Harford County, only 4 in Howard, and, in Montgomery, only 9 out of more than 29,000. There was no reason to suspect fraud on the basis of the number of forms returned or the reasons identified when the returns were investigated.

Test of the Accuracy of Voter-Notification Delivery. What was more difficult to determine was whether voter-notification forms had been delivered to persons who did not reside at the addresses indicated or to fictitious persons. The authors devised a simple check that was implemented in Maryland with the cooperation of the Maryland State Administrative Board of Election Laws.

A list of 500 fictitious names was drawn up which consisted of 250 male and 250 female first names combined with 500 uncommon last names. The last names were selected from the Washington, D. C. telephone book from among names which appeared no more than seven times; no last name was combined with the first name with which it appeared in the book. These names were matched with 500 actual addresses in the five jurisdictions having mail registration, also selected from telephone directories. Of these, 396 were multi-family dwellings and 104 single-family dwellings. Again, a check was made to ensure that no name at an address resembled the fictitious name to be associated with that address. The addresses were scattered through Baltimore City, Montgomery, and Prince George's counties, in as broad a geographical cross section as possible. There was no attempt to concentrate on highly transient sections, rooming houses, or areas where mail delivery may be suspect, but the ratio of multi-family to single-family residences was based on the assumption that multi-family residence addresses would be more likely to be used by persons who wished to "pad the registration rolls." Further, it was assumed that incorrect single-family residence addresses are more likely to be spotted by polling place judges. At least one guilty plea for false registration using a private residence address occurred in 1974 in Santa Ana, California; seven other persons have been charged with false registration and voting in that area.

These 500 fictitious persons were sent a first-class mailing which consisted of an outdated treasurer's report form in an official state board envelope. If the fraud protection system worked perfectly, all 500 envelopes should have been returned. The result of the mailing is shown in Table 20.

Table 20

RESULTS OF TEST MAILING TO FICTITIOUS PERSONS IN MARYLAND MAIL-REGISTRATION COUNTIES [a]

	Number of Mailings Sent	Returned in Three Weeks	Not Returned in Three Weeks	Percent Not Returned
Baltimore City				
Multi-family	145	137	8	5.5
Single-family	39	20	19	48.7
Total	184	157	27	14.7
Montgomery County				
Multi-family	112	105	7	6.2
Single-family	31	25	6	19.3
Total	143	130	13	9.0
Prince George's County				
Multi-family	127	120	7	5.5
Single-family	28	24	4	14.2
Total	155	144	11	7.0
Harford County				
Multi-family	6	5	1	16.6
Single-family	3	2	1	33.3
Total	9	7	2	22.2
Howard County				
Multi-family	6	6	0	0
Single-family	3	3	0	0
Total	9	9	0	0
All jurisdictions				
Multi-family	396	373	23	5.8
Single-family	104	74	30	28.8
Total	500	447	53	10.6

[a] The test mailing used first-class postage and an official Maryland State Administrative Board of Election Laws envelope.

This test was not intended to be conclusive. Rather it was an attempt to determine whether it would be possible to place a large number of fraudulent voters on the registration lists without this fact being obvious to the local registration officials. If the voter-notification form is not returned by the post office, the registrars have no reason to question the validity of the registration. Approximately 10 percent of the first-class letters mailed in official government envelopes to fictitious persons were not returned within a twenty-one-day period, and it is reasonable to assume that this figure would increase if commonplace names and areas of transient population were used. Under these circumstances a small conspiracy involving residents of large apartment complexes might be highly successful.

Even when the voter-notification card is returned to the registrar, however, the name of the registrants may not be removed immediately from the rolls. Near the close of the registration period in a populous county, particularly, sheer lack of time may prevent the removal of the name from the rolls prior to the election. In Maryland the name of a fraudulent voter registered in the manner described above may remain on the books for up to five years. In New Jersey, however, his name probably would be removed after a sample ballot addressed to him was returned by the postal service as undeliverable.

If nothing else, this test indicates that the possibility of registering fraudulently and voting does exist in spite of the mail-notification-form check. Further verification of registration lists, if only spot checks, is probably desirable.

Misuse of Voter-Registration Cards. The voter-identification card, or voter-notification card, as it is sometimes called, has been used as personal identification for a variety of nonelection purposes. It has been credited as such on the assumption that possession of the voter-notification card implies that the bearer has satisfied a local government official that he is an American citizen, over eighteen years of age, who resides at the address indicated. Each of these characteristics—citizenship, age, and residence—has been exploited in the misuse of the voter-notification card.

Perhaps the most serious misuse of the card was reported in New Jersey, where it was alleged that aliens illegally in the country had registered to vote and subsequently used their voter-identification cards as "proof of citizenship" in obtaining employment. This is exceptionally easy to do in New Jersey because, by rule, a person is not required to declare his place of birth, date of birth, or, if relevant, date and place of naturalization in order to register. This abuse has been reported elsewhere in the country, too. Voter-identification cards are sometimes offered as evidence of citizenship by persons passing between Canada and the United States. Election officials report that this type of voter-registration fraud is extremely difficult to detect because persons engaging in the deception for the purpose of claiming American citizenship do not vote at all, and may retain and use voter-identification cards for this purpose indefinitely.

The voter-registration card has also been used by persons under the age of eighteen in both Maryland and New Jersey for the purpose of obtaining alcoholic beverages. In Union and Burlington counties, New Jersey, persons under eighteen have used the voter-identification card as proof of age to obtain the alcoholic-beverage card issued by the county clerks. A similar violation was uncovered in Baltimore City when a seventeen-year-old was called for jury duty. The fact that he was underage was discovered when the court attempted to obtain an explanation for his failure to appear. There was no prosecution because the youth had not indicated his age on the original mail-registration form, and the supplementary form, which did contain the false age, lacked other essentials necessary to secure a conviction.

As a result of this event, the attorney general of Maryland recommended that each local board take steps to prevent recurrences. Recommended actions included printing the words "Not Valid for Identification or Proof of Age" on the voter-notification card. Local boards were also asked to notify their local boards of liquor license commissioners and ask their cooperation. In neither Maryland nor New Jersey is the voter-identification card valid proof of age. Tavern owners in both states have objected, claiming that if the card is issued by the state and is honored by the state for voting purposes, it should also be honored by the state for drinking purposes. Maryland introduced legislation in 1975 to change the name of the voter-notification card from "Identification Card" to "Notification Card." This matter was the subject of an urgent "priority notice" from the state board of elections to all local boards of elections.

The voter-registration card has been used to prove residence in Florida for the purpose of obtaining a fishing license, and for exemption from state taxes permitted to homesteaders. The most bizarre use of the voter-identification card was reported from Pensacola, Florida, where vagrants known to sell their blood for money to buy wine were told that they could not do so without personal identification. They were advised to obtain voter-registration cards and did so, which enabled them to continue selling their blood and, presumably, replenishing their supply of wine.

Voter-registration cards may be used as personal identification by persons charged with misdemeanors. In Dade County, Florida, a person arrested for a misdemeanor may be released from custody upon posting $1 bond and his voter-registration card. It has been alleged that prostitutes register several times under different names to escape being held overnight and to avoid records of multiple arrest. On the other hand, this use of the voter-registration card protects people from the bail bondsman if they are arrested on minor charges, according to Dade County officials.

SUMMARY AND CONCLUSION

Mail registration provides an added convenience to persons who wish to register and vote. By itself, it does not necessarily increase voter registration. The standard pattern in most states—high registration in presidential election years, low registration in nonpresidential election years—confirms the fact that voter interest in the offices and candidates on the ballot, and in the issues, is a far more important factor than the method of voter registration in determining how many names are on the registry. No appreciable increase in voter turnout was related to mail registration. Persons who registered by mail during 1974 voted in approximately the same percentages as other registered voters.

The relationship between mail registration and party identification is inconclusive. Maryland, a heavily Democratic state, registers voters by political party but New Jersey does not. Evidence does suggest that persons who register by mail are less likely to affiliate with either party, and that the increase in "declines" in Maryland in 1974 reduced Republican more than Democratic registration.

The cost of registering by mail seems to be about $1.00 per registered voter. This figure covers the postage-paid registration form, printing and processing, voter-registration lists, and polling place rosters. Variations from a low of fifty cents to a high of $2.00 were reported. Mail registration will definitely decrease the cost of voter registration in Maryland and New Jersey if it *replaces* rather than merely supplements the current system. Maryland and New Jersey now have expensive personal registration systems which remain partially in effect.

Anticipated administrative problems arising from duplicate registrations, illegible handwriting, and difficulty in locating certain types of addresses for assignment to election districts or precincts have proven to be minor and manageable in Maryland and New Jersey.

There is a potential for vote fraud under the mail-registration system. The safeguards written into the law are stronger than those actually implemented in practice. They include a witness to the signature (New Jersey only); a voter-notification form mailed to the address of the registrant which, if undeliverable as addressed, is returned to the election office; a signature check at the polling place; dissemination of voter-registration lists to interested persons and political parties; periodic purges of the voter rolls; and small precinct size. Not all of these safeguards are in effect in all counties or in each state, however. Mail registration combined with absentee voting might be exploited in a type of vote fraud which would be very difficult to detect.

Voter-registration fraud has been perpetrated for non-voting purposes. Individuals have obtained voter-registration cards for use as official identification, to establish citizenship for employment, age for drinking, or residence for purposes of avoiding taxes or fees.

Maryland and New Jersey officials in general support the concept of voter registration by mail. Few, however, favor federal legislation on mail registration. Most were very critical of the proposed mass distribution of federal mail registration forms to every household. Robert S. Raymar, of the Office of the Governor of New Jersey, considered this proposal "an enormous waste of money." [10] He estimated that it would cost more than $150,000 merely to print enough forms for New Jersey alone. This is more than $1.00 for every voter who actually registered in New Jersey in 1974. Other officials expressed concern that national legislation would supersede state legislation and might contain even fewer security checks. Officials in both states pointed out that voter-registration forms in their states are now readily available by telephone request, in public places, and, in New Jersey, even in newspapers.

Mail registration, if adopted by the states, poses no problem of dual voter-registration systems. If congressional legislation is passed, states will have to determine whether to abolish registration entirely for federal elections, maintain dual systems of voter registration, or adopt the federal system for state elections. As this study shows, many methods of mail registration are possible. Although each can increase voter convenience, though not necessarily total registration, each could conceivably increase the incidence of fraud.

---

[10] Interview with Robert S. Raymar by the author, State Capitol, 13 January 1975.

Administrative procedures for implementing any system of voter registration by mail must protect the integrity of the system as well as the convenience of the voter.

As Joseph P. Harris stated:

> An honest electoral system lies at the very basis of popular government. Without it popular government is polluted at its very source. The public morale is weakened if not destroyed. Citizens lose confidence in their governments. Corruption is invited.[11]

Voter-registration and voter-identification systems, however devised and implemented, must be capable of preserving the security of the ballot from the very few who would exploit any weakness to seize political power.

---

[11] Harris, *Registration of Voters in the United States*, p. 1.

LIBRARY OF DAVIDSON COLLEGE

Books on two week loan may be checked out for **two weeks.** Books must be brought to the Circulation Desk in order to be renewed.

_____ per date due.

_____ ject to special regulations at the discretion of